OH WHAT A TANGLED WEB WE WEAVE...

Copyright © 2023 Jim Freund
All Rights Reserved
ISBN: 9798865936244

PREFACE, ACKNOWLEDGEMENTS AND DEDICATION

After writing about 35 short stories during retirement, I took a shot at my first novella last year. *The Gold-Plated Years* began with a nod to one of my short stories that closed with things up in the air, and then went on to explore what happened to the protagonist in the several months thereafter.

I liked that concept, so I've done it again in this, my second novella. Set in the late 1970's, it builds on the short story *Sex, Lies and Private Eyes*, which left the two main characters in seeming disarray, and then examines how they deal with their continuing problem over the next two years.

The title of this novella – *Oh what a tangled web we weave* – is the first half of a couplet by Sir Walter Scott, which concludes with the words, "when first we practice to deceive." The theme of both the original short story and the novella is to illustrate what a dangerous course a prevaricator sets out on when concocting the first lie, with all the sub-falsehoods and diversions then needed to buttress the basic untruth. Needless to say, neither the law firm nor any character is intended to resemble any past or present firm or anyone living or dead.

Let me acknowledge the insightful cover illustration of my long-time collaborator, Joe Azar; the superb textual editing by my friend, John Doyle; and special thanks to my colleague Raymond for his many contributions to the final product.

As for a dedication, I continue to turn to my wonderful wife Barbara – the love of my life – for her consistent and much needed support.

I hope you enjoy *Oh What a Tangled Web We Weave*.

November 2023   Jim Freund

OH WHAT A TANGLED WEB WE WEAVE . . .

I

"Okay," said Cliff Cook, "let's get this meeting underway." He made a gesture to the several executives of Seacrest Corp. seated at the long table, who responded to their CEO with attentive expressions.

It's a lovely Fall day in 1977. Earlier this year, Jimmy Carter took over as U.S. President, Elvis Presley died at age 42, and New York City – which is where Seacrest is located – endured a 25-hour blackout.

"I think you all know our lawyer, Jack Lawrence, from the Jenkins & Price firm. Jack has been handling our litigation for a number of years now, and very capably, I might add."

Jack acknowledged the compliment with a modest smile and a mock salute, though he considered it fully justified. He did feel he had done a lot of good work for Cook's company, and in the process, Seacrest had become his most significant client.

Jack, in his mid 40's, stood 5 foot 10 and was physically fit although bulging a bit around the midriff. His gray-flecked hair receded slightly on his forehead, and his pleasant features fell just short of handsome.

Jack was an important, well-regarded, mid-level litigation partner in the NYC firm of Jenkins & Price, or J&P as the staff usually referred to it. The firm had about 60 lawyers, of which 20 were partners. Jack was the chairman of the New Partner Recommendation Committee, which identified partner candidate each year for the full complement of partners to vote on.

"Thanks for the plug, Cliff," Jack replied. "And this young man seated to my right is Kevin Dodge, one of our premier associates, who will be working with me on this case, his first for Seacrest."

Jack was, in fact, quite pleased that Kevin Dodge had been assigned to him for what promised to be an arduous assignment. The two of them had worked together several times before, representing other clients, and Jack found Kevin to be bright, articulate and diligent. He was also aware, although he usually didn't notice such things, that Kevin was quite good-looking – a handsome face capped by a shock of jet black hair. Jack viewed him as a litigation star-in-the-making, almost certain to become a partner when he came up for consideration in about a year.

Jack mused. *I need someone like Kevin to help me handle Cliff, who is a very demanding client. But I'll say this for Cook – unlike some other clients, if you perform well, there's no trouble with the fees. So far, I've been sitting pretty.*

Speaking of sitting pretty, seated across the table from Kevin and Jack was Emma Searles, Seacrest's General Counsel. She was a very attractive young woman – face, figure, brains, the works. Emma reminded Jack of a young woman he had wooed in San Diego back in his Navy days – the woman who broke his novice Ensign's heart when she passed him over for a grizzled war hero Lieutenant Commander . . . .

Jack had long suspected there was more going on

between Cliff Cook and Emma Searles than a purely professional relationship. It wasn't simply that Cliff made sure she was present at every meeting, even if the subject was out of her bailiwick.

> Jack mused. *There is just something different about their interaction . . . . But I don't know for sure, and Cook has a wife and family. I've never been too observant as to that kind of thing. Women – like my wife Brenda – are a lot more perceptive and intuitive. And I certainly never felt it was my place to inquire further.*
>
> *Not only that – I just don't condone a married man having an affair outside his marriage. Brenda and I have been married for 18 years; and even though we've been going through a rough patch the last few years, I would never do what Cliff is apparently doing. And Brenda and I don't even have any kids, while Cliff and Cynthia have two teenagers, which makes what he seems to be up to seem even worse . . . .*

Fred Grant, Seacrest's chief financial officer, began to describe the new case. Seacrest was preparing to sue a company named Congruent that had sold a subsidiary to Seacrest a year ago. The subsidiary's financial soundness, it turned out, had been seriously inflated, and thus Seacrest had overpaid for the acquisition.

Kevin was taking part in the discussion, and at one point, broke in to ask, "What measure of damages are we going to be able to prove here? Can we produce a good record of how we went about valuing the deal, in order to justify a hefty multiplier effect on the disappearing earnings?"

Before Fred Grant had a chance to reply, Emma spoke up, in a warm husky voice. "Good question, Kevin. In fact, it's the key to the entire case. Let me describe what we have on this, as well as what I wish we had but can't seem to lay our hands on".

Listening to the dialogue that then ensued between Emma and Kevin, Jack focused entirely on the substance of what was said, ignoring any sparks that may have been flying.

* * *

[Emma musing] *Hey, I'm Emma, and I play an important role in this tale, so you should hear my side of things directly from the source.*

I remember the day it started to unwind – the day Jack Lawrence brought Kevin Dodge over to that first meeting on the Congruent case. I was attracted to Kevin – good-looking, smart, and obviously on-the-make. He reminded me a little of John Travolta in "Saturday Night Fever". But I might have been less receptive if things had been going better with Cliff. In fact, just the previous night he and I had done battle in his office . . . . Let me repeat the dialogue.

"Now, Emma, about the Congruent case...."

"Goddamit, Cliff, forget the goddamn case. I want to talk about us. I want to know whether you've told your wife that you're leaving her."

"Oh come on, don't be so unreasonable...."

"Me, unreasonable? I'll tell you what's unreasonable. Spending Thanksgiving by myself, munching on a turkey TV-dinner, watching a Detroit Lions game – while you, Madame Cynthia and those adorable kids of yours warmed each other around the family hearth, sipping hot apple cider."

"I'm sorry, Emma –"

"I don't need your sympathy – I want us together. And out in the open. This is no life for me. Whenever we're together it's always in hiding. I'm sick of skulking around. I want you to leave your wife and marry me."

He patted my hand – like you'd soothe a little kid – and said, "Look, Emma, I understand your frustration. I love you very much, but it's very difficult to leave a wife of 20 years and abandon two children. Rest assured, I'm working on it – trying to get over the hump."

"Hah! – the hump that's about to be over for you is the one that's been taking place in my bed!"

And I proceeded to stomp out of his office, slamming the door behind me. I was mad as hell – not just putting on an act, although maybe a little over the top. But that's what's necessary in dealing with Cliff, who has to be pushed hard to do anything. Whatever I'd been saying hadn't worked. So when I met Kevin, I must have realized it was time to consider other possibilities.

One occurred the evening after our first meeting. Kevin and I were alone in my office, sitting next to each other at a small round table, working on the Congruent case. I've fixed up my office with a lot of personal touches – I wouldn't call it a boudoir, but it's not your everyday stylized executive quarters.

Kevin said, "Here's the way I see the carve-out from the indemnification provision – " but I interrupted him.

"Let's take a little break from the case, Kevin. Tell me about yourself. Are you a native New Yorker? Where did you go to college? Is there a Mrs. Dodge?"

Kevin leaned back and replied to my three questions – yes, Dartmouth, and no. Then, after offering a brief summary of his life, he asked me about myself. I replied in kind. It turned out we had both graduated from different law schools – me from Penn, he from Cornell – at the same time five years ago in '72.

"If I may be so bold to ask," said Kevin in a playful voice, "how did someone so youthful get to be General Counsel of a behemoth like Seacrest?"

I fluttered my eyelashes – a habit I picked up in high school and haven't been able to shake since – and replied, "I take it that what you mean by that incredibly rude question is – who did I have to screw to get this job?"

> Kevin leaned back, put his palms on the table, and said, "I'm going to let that one pass."
>
> I reached out and placed my hand on top of his. "As we get to know each other better, Kevin, maybe I'll explain it to you."
>
> For just a moment, Kevin put his other hand on top of mine. With my free hand, I blew him a kiss . . . .

* * *

The next all-hands meeting on the Congruent case took place three days later in the Seacrest conference room. Cliff Cook wasn't there, so Fred Grant and Emma Searles were leading the discussion.

As the meeting progressed, Jack began to get an uncomfortable feeling that something not purely professional was going on between Emma and Kevin. He noticed that when either of them talked, the words were directed right at the other – accompanied by certain penetrating looks. This had the effect of virtually excluding the rest of the people in the room. Their discourse was sprinkled with shared references and double entendres – the kind of thing not usually heard in a litigation conference room.

At one point, for example, in trying to underline the distinction between whether Congruent's misstatements had been intentionally fraudulent or just negligent, Kevin quipped, "It's like the difference between rape and everyday intercourse." Emma replied, without missing a beat, "Sometimes, it's not so easy to tell the difference" – to which Kevin winked and said, "Touché."

Jack promptly retreated into his traditional turtle mode – trying to ignore the byplay, or at least to explain it away. But a new worry struck him.

> *If I'm correct in my suspicion that Emma and Cliff Cook are romantically linked, it would be disastrous for Jenkins & Price if the client were to catch a J&P associate trying to cut in on the CEO's girl – to say nothing of the ethical implications.*

Notwithstanding the visible evidence, Jack went back into denial. That is, until a few days later, when Jack had an early morning flight to catch and wanted to speak to Kevin before getting on the plane. At 6:30 a.m. Jack put in a call to Kevin's home number. It was answered on the third ring by a sleepy female voice which sounded familiar. "Yes?"

Jack said, "May I please speak to Kevin."

Jack then heard the same voice, now turned away from the mouthpiece, say, "Oh shit, Kevin, wake up. I thought I was home and picked up your line by mistake. Someone wants you – I'm putting the phone on the pillow."

This time, Jack realized there was no mistaking the husky tones of Emma Searles. . . .

* * *

[Emma musing] *Well, after my stupid mistake this morning with Kevin's phone, I realized Jack Lawrence probably knows what's up, which raises the question – is he likely to run to Cliff with the news? I seriously doubt it. Jack doesn't seem like that kind of guy – and the risk is minimized* because the other offending party is one of his own associates!

But hey, do I really care whether Cliff finds out about me and Kevin? Or, to take matters a step further, maybe I want Cliff to know? I'm so mad at him. He just takes me for granted. Nothing I've said or done so far has shaken him up enough to leave his wife. Maybe this will do the trick.

It's not that I don't realize this is risky business, but I guess I'm willing to take the chance. Almost everything in my life up to this point has been a gamble which I've usually won. And besides, Kevin really turns me on in a way that Cliff never has – although it's true that he lacks Cliff's stature and bankroll. Maybe Kevin isn't my long-term cup of tea, but for now he really suits my purpose. I'll play it out for a while and see where things go . . . .

* * *

When Jack returned the next day from the business trip, he summoned Kevin Dodge into his office.

"Look, Kevin," he said, "I don't like to interfere in the personal lives of my associates, but I can't continue to turn a blind eye here. I'm worried about what it might mean for the firm. I'm going to ask you a few questions, and I want you to be absolutely straight with me. "

Seated in a chair across the desk from Jack, Kevin had a look of concern – but not panic – on his face.

Jack decided to start out in a formal mode, like the tone of a judicial opinion. "Based on the following facts – my hearing, at 6:30 a.m., a voice on your home phone that I recognized as belonging to Emma Searles; that voice calling out your name; and her remark about leaving the phone on the pillow – I've concluded that you're having an intimate relationship with Emma. Am I right?

"You're right," replied Kevin, evenly.

"Am I also correct in my suspicion that Emma is Cliff Cook's mistress?"

"Well, the term you're using is a little old-fashioned, but if you're asking whether they've been engaged in a long-term affair, then – at least according to what Emma has told me – you're correct."

"And I take it that Cook doesn't yet know about you and Emma?"

"As far as I know, he doesn't."

Jack stood up to give his next words added emphasis. "Well then, you've simply got to break this off with Emma before you endanger the firm's relations with Seacrest. If Cook were to find out about it, he'd be mad as hell – and rightly so. In fact, he'd likely show us the door. And I've worked too hard to get to where we are with Seacrest – I'm not about to risk screwing it up."

Kevin paused before replying. He had obviously anticipated this confrontation and prepared himself for it, as a good lawyer does.

"Jack, I hear what you're saying, I understand your concern, and I consider it entirely appropriate for you to bring it up. Here's the thing, though. As far as I'm concerned, I'd be willing to end this relationship with Emma. She's a tantalizing woman, that's for sure, but I'm not taking it too seriously – and there are plenty of other fish in the sea . But there's a downside to my breaking this off which you ought to consider."

"What's that?" Jack snapped, immediately suspicious of Kevin's motives.

"Emma is more into our fling than I am. I'd like to think that's because she considers me a great lover, but I'm pretty sure there's another reason. She wants Cliff to leave his wife for her. I suspect she's using me to get back at him. Either way, it comes down to the same thing.

"If I break off with her abruptly, and for no discernible reason, she might think that our firm is pulling the strings. She could then get mad as hell at Jenkins & Price. And this woman wields a lot of power at Seacrest. She could get us fired just like that" – here he snapped his fingers – "without ever telling Cook the real reason."

Jack could see that Kevin had a point, although by no means a conclusive one. "So what are you saying?"

"That we've got a better chance of staying on as Seacrest's counsel if I continue the fling with Emma and only gradually extricate myself."

"Yeah, right," replied Jack in a cynical tone – "it's tough work but someone has to do it . . . . Still I'm worried that Cook will find out."

"Don't worry, I'll be discreet."

But it wasn't Kevin's discretion Jack was worried about – it was Emma's, especially if she were trying to get back at Cliff. . . .

Still not convinced this was the right course to take, but unable to come up with a better solution – and knowing he wasn't too good at this kind of stuff – Jack gave Kevin the benefit of the doubt, while emphasizing the need to take due care.

* * *

Watching Kevin at an all-hands meeting at Seacrest a few days later, Jack couldn't fault his behavior. As for Emma – she was something else entirely. Even though Cliff Cook was right there in the room, Emma managed to do something provocative whenever he was distracted for a moment. At one point, for instance, she slid a sheet of paper across to Kevin which Jack could see contained doodles of hearts. When they passed by each other at the coffee machine, she patted Kevin on the rear end. And there was much fluttering of eyelashes.

Jack couldn't tell whether Cliff noticed any of this. But he realized that as the case moved forward, and with Emma acting so daring – almost as if she wanted to get caught in the act – it was only a matter of time before Cliff woke up to what was going on. So Jack decided that the situation called for a more drastic step.

Throughout his professional life, Jack had encountered situations like this one – where the truth could hurt, and a little shading of the truth eased the pain. At such moments of internal conflict, he habitually tuned in to an inner voice that he'd dubbed – mindful of the alliteration – his *Pal*. The inner voice could usually be counted on to offer shrewd counsel, albeit a bit opinionated for Jack's taste and often inclined to undue rationalization. He often took *Pal's* advice, except when other factors *Pal* hadn't considered came into play.

Jack now issued a silent summons. "Hey, *Pal*, wake up – I've got a ripe one for you."

Pal went right to work and together they came up with a workable plan that Jack decided to follow. Later that day he called Kevin into his office to broach it.

"I know, I know. . ." said Kevin as he entered the room, before Jack could even open his mouth.

Jack came right to the point. "Look, Kevin, after that scene this morning – which I concede was not your fault – I've decided to replace you on the Congruent case with Jill Marsh. If you feel the need to keep your affair going with Emma temporarily, then do so – but strictly on an outside-the-office basis. Cliff Cook is much less likely to catch on if the two of you aren't playing grab-ass in his conference room."

Kevin pondered this for a moment. "Well, I'll admit it was getting uncomfortable for me in there, so I'm okay with your idea – provided it doesn't look like I'm getting fired."

Pal had anticipated this reaction on Kevin's part and prepared Jack's plan to deal with it. "That's fair enough. I'll say to Cliff and Emma that a client of the firm you've been servicing for several years just got sued on a deal you know a lot about. In view of your past knowledge, the client specifically requested your services. You're not yet so deep into the Congruent case – I'll try to resist adding that you're apparently quite deep into something else – so we're replacing you on the Congruent team. To make it more palatable to them, we won't charge Seacrest for the time you've put in on the case up to now, nor for the time necessary to bring Jill up to speed."

Kevin nodded in approval. "That's pretty ingenious. But I'd like to try it out on Emma first before you announce it publicly."

"No way. I don't want her to say 'no,' at which point we'd be proceeding over her objection. It's better to present Seacrest with a *fait accompli*. Okay, let's get going . . . ."

This fake story about another client requiring Kevin's services seemed innocent enough to Jack at the time – in his view, it was "just a little professional lubricant to make things go down smoothly." And he was proud of his pragmatic "no double charge" idea to make the substitution more palatable, which he – not *Pal* – had come up with on his own.

But what he didn't realize until after relating it to Kevin was that he couldn't tell that same story to Jill Marsh, or to anyone else at his firm for that matter, because they would know there was no such other client.

So, later that day in his office, when he told Jill she was going to be working on the Congruent case, Jack had to come up with a different bogus explanation, which he did (with *Pal's* help).

Jack started out this way. "Look, Jill, let me be perfectly candid." (He didn't warn her that he frequently counseled associates to *watch out when somebody begins that way!*) "I sense a certain chemistry problem between Kevin and the Seacrest people, which is likely to get worse as time goes by. Although they haven't met you, I'm sure you'll be a much better fit. But I can't really say that to Seacrest – and I don't want to embarrass Kevin by making it seem he's being ousted. So I'm going to tell them a little white lie about Kevin's services being required for one of his long-term clients. Are you okay with that?"

"No problem," said Jill, who seemed pleased at getting involved in a major case and uninterested in the cover story.

So that's the way Jack played it the next day at Seacrest's office with Kevin not in attendance. Cliff and Emma registered some surprise. But with Jill now sitting right there, basking in Jack's enthusiastic description of her skills – and in light of the "no charge" fee adjustment Jack proffered with some flair – there wasn't much they could say on the spot by way of objection.

* * *

[Emma musing] *The news that Jenkins & Price had taken Kevin off the Congruent case really caught me by surprise, so I didn't react at the meeting. But my mind went to work on it later that morning.*

Once the initial shock wore off, I was mad as hell at Kevin for not warning me about what was happening.. Given our intimacy, you'd think he would have done that. But then, as I pondered it further, I realized that Jack may have put him under wraps. And I began to wonder whether that "other client" story was true or just an excuse Jack used to get Kevin off the case. The timing was simply too convenient – and I had seen the disapproving look on Jack's face when I was flirting with Kevin in the conference room....

I realized I was going to miss having Kevin around the office. The heart doodles, the pat on his ass – I knew what I was doing. And I wanted Cliff to notice that something was up – just enough to make him jealous and uneasy, but without forcing him to do anything extreme.

Another thing gnawed at me. The Congruent case gave Kevin and me a great excuse to be together – not only in public, but privately too, and late at night in my office. If Cliff had stumbled upon the two of us, I had a built-in excuse for Kevin's presence.

And then my mind went into high gear, along these lines. Seacrest is a major Jenkins & Price client. We don't have to stand for this. We had Kevin first – let's fight to get him back. Since Jack knows I have a "special interest" in the matter, it would be stronger if the "we want Kevin back" plea came from Cliff. I figured I could arrange that without him becoming unduly suspicious....

A few days later, Cliff Cook called Jack to say he was coming over to his law office – an occurrence unusual enough to cause some trepidation on Jack's part.

When Cliff arrived at Jenkins & Price, he skipped any small talk. "Let me get right to the point, Jack. Emma and I are unhappy that you took Kevin Dodge off the Congruent case. Jill Marsh is affable enough, and I'm sure she's a competent lawyer, but we both feel that Kevin is a lot more capable and experienced. He's a very special guy, we had him first, and we want him back."

This presented Jack with a real problem. Still, he was amused at the irony of Cliff Cook pleading for the return to duty of the young man who was banging his girlfriend! The good news for Jack was that, at least to this point, Cliff evidently had no idea something was up between Emma and Kevin.

"I'll see what I can do, Cliff," said Jack," although I think I'm powerless in this instance – it was a Jenkins & Price decision. But listen, Jill Marsh is a very good associate – just be patient for a week or so while she gets up to speed. And I promise you I'll spend more of my own time on the case than ever before."

Cliff seemed somewhat assuaged by this. But then, just as he appeared ready to leave, he said, "Jack, there's something else I want to talk to you about – a personal problem unrelated to the Congruent case."

With those words – even though Cliff delivered them as a casual afterthought – Jack realized that what he was about to hear was the real reason for Cliff's visit to his office.

"Jack, I know we've never talked about this subject, but by now you've probably figured out that Emma and I have been engaged in a long-term intimate relationship."

Jack's guard immediately went up and he summoned *Pal* without delay. This was the last subject he wanted to be discussing with Cook. He followed *Pal's* quick advice and murmured something unintelligible in reply, which neither confirmed nor denied his knowledge.

Cliff went on. "Even though I'm happily married and at heart a family man, my relations with Emma have assumed a very important role in my life – one that I find immensely satisfying. But lately, Emma has been different. In the past, she was always available to me, but now she sometimes claims she's busy. I'll spare you the gory details, but the sex – which was incomparable – just isn't the same. She's become testy and irritable, mainly on the issue of me leaving my wife – even though Emma has been well aware I'd never do that while my kids are still in their early teens. In short, I have a hunch she's seeing someone else on the side."

Jack's insides began to rumble, but he made a real effort to keep his facial expression neutral – not wanting an inadvertent glimmer to betray his level of knowledge. But why, he wondered, is Cliff telling me this? He soon found out.

"Jack, I need to find out what's going on. You're my most trusted advisor. I want you to hire a private detective to observe Emma's every move over the next two weeks. I'm determined to get to the bottom of this. But, needless to say, Emma can't have any idea what's happening. And should she suspect something is up, I don't want my fingerprints to appear. Got it? Okay, go to work."

With that – and before Jack could respond – Cliff rose from his chair and strode out of the office.

After Cook left, Jack sat there in shock – silently musing with *Pal* about what to do next.

> *I know I have to hire the private eye – that's a direct order from the client. But how about before that? What I really want to do is tell Kevin about the detective, let him tell Emma, and then insist they cool it while Sam Spade goes about his thing. But Cliff was insistent that Emma not know about this – I can't violate that direct order of confidentiality.*

At this point, *Pal* took over, and his awesome ability to rationalize even the most egregious conduct became the dominant voice in Jack's head. He found himself reasoning that this didn't mean he couldn't tell *Kevin* about it, as long as Kevin promised not to pass the word along to Emma. The justification for this was that Cliff hadn't said anything specific about *that* – a justification conveniently overlooking the fact that Cook wasn't aware Jack knew the identity of Emma's playmate. Still, Jack wondered whether he could rely on Kevin not to tell Emma, since Kevin wasn't the one Cook put that burden on – Jack was.

> *But even assuming Kevin will preserve the secret – for which I plan to extract his solemn vow – the question is whether he'll be able to induce Emma to stay away for the duration of the detective's investigation. She's a very determined woman . . . .*

Then *Pal* hit upon what Jack considered a clever scheme (albeit completely failing to reckon how it caused him to plunge even deeper into the morass). Later that afternoon Jack broached the plan to Kevin in the partner's office.

"I had a visit from Cliff Cook today. The bad news is that he knows something is up with Emma, because he asked me to hire a private detective to tail her for the next few weeks. So, obviously, you two have to cool it during that time. The good news is that he obviously doesn't suspect you're the problem, because he began by asking me to bring you back onto the Congruent case. I'm going to tell him that's impossible, but we've still got the detective problem. And you can't say anything about that to Emma, because Cliff was very insistent that this not get back to her. You have got to promise me that you won't tell Emma."

Kevin thought for a moment before replying. "I'm willing to make that promise – but if I can't tell her, what will I say is the reason we have to cool it?"

"I've thought about that – *actually Pal had come up with the notion* – and here's my idea. I'm going to send you to England for a fortnight, as they say. Get you the hell out of here. That way, there'll be nothing for the detective to discover."

"But what do I say to Emma?"

"Well, she thinks you left the Congruent case to work for another Jenkins & Price client. So just tell her you have to go to London to depose or interview some key witnesses in that other case."

"I guess that'll work . . . . But what are you going to do about Cliff wanting me to come back on Congruent?" "I'll just tell him I tried my darndest but can't extricate you from that other case. But I'm not going to say anything to him about your going to London – there's no need for him to know that."

Kevin pondered Jack's plan. His next question was, "What will I do over there?"

"I've considered that – *in fact, Jack had indeed come up with this idea himself, without any help from Pal.* You might as well be productive. For a while now, Jenkins & Price has been secretly considering opening a London office to service some of our multinational clients. I'm one of the partners in charge of the project. We haven't made a final decision yet, but while you're over there, you could scout out possible locations. Since we're still undecided, we don't want our associates to know we're even thinking about a London office. So you can't tell anyone what you're doing over there. Just leave town – don't talk about it. Let them think you're on vacation."

Kevin frowned. "What if someone – like another client – asks my secretary about my whereabouts?"

"Just tell her to say, 'He's out of town' – with no elaboration."

Kevin appeared uncomfortable with the proposed deception, but Jack had no hesitation about it and even confessed his current feelings to *Pal*:

> *I hate to admit this, but I'm so wound up in the scheme that I almost feel a sense of exhilaration. I'm really on a roll, with three or four fabrications working at different levels. And I'm not even through yet . . . .*

Jack went on with his instructions. "Now Kevin, you have to tell Emma not to phone you over there – and you can't call her, either at her home or her office, since the detective will probably be tapping those lines."

Kevin frowned. "What will I tell her is the reason we can't talk on the phone?"

"You have to figure that out, but remember, you can't mention the private eye. Try blaming it on yourself – maybe something to do with the other case you're working on, a fear that your adversary may be investigating *you*...."

Jack never really resolved all the loose ends. After Kevin left the office, he sat there very much alone. The temporary sense of exhilaration had passed, and all he could see was how much deeper he was sinking into this quagmire.

A famous quote – often attributed to Shakespeare but actually from Sir Walter Scott – came to him. *What a tangled web we weave, when first we practice to deceive* . . . . Worse still, he couldn't avoid some nagging ethical questions, such as whether he was violating an obligation to his client by impeding the detective's investigation.

His ruminations were broken by a call he needed to take on another matter. As he picked up the phone, he thought *What the hell, the next move is to hire the detective.* At this point, *Pal* chimed in, adding this hiring caveat: *He certainly should be competent, but he needn't be, shall we say, world-class . . . .*

* * *

[Emma musing] *Life has become really boring with Kevin over in London, and not even calling me. I miss him – and I also miss the chance to pressure Cliff. Since I'm an activist by nature, I need to do something about this situation. . . .*

The next few days were relatively quiet. The private detective Jack hired was on the job, but with Kevin in London and out of touch with Emma, there was nothing for him to discover. It began to look to Jack like he'd dodged the bullet.

That temporary state of euphoria was shattered the next afternoon, at a meeting with the Seacrest people. Cliff was there, but not Emma. "Will Emma be joining us?" Jack asked him.

"Oh, Emma left town last evening. She had to make a trip to London to put out a fire at our subsidiary over there."

* * *

[Emma musing] *It was, in retrospect, sort of delicious. The flight over was first class. When I arrived in London the next morning, Kevin had gone out to have breakfast. I told the desk clerk at Kevin's hotel that I was his wife and was slipping into town to surprise him on his birthday. The clerk let me in to Kevin's room.*

At the airport, I'd bought a large towel decorated with the British flag. I took off my clothes, wrapped myself in the towel, and lay down on the bed. When Kevin opened the door, I began to sing, "There'll always be an England," as I slowly unfurled the flag . . . .

Kevin was obviously glad to see me. But he did seem concerned that if and when Jack found out I'd crossed the pond, the partner might think his associate cooked up the rendezvous. I let him stew over that for a few minutes and then steered him in a more productive direction . . . .

* * *

When Jack got back to the office, he called Kevin in London to tell him Emma was on her way to London. "I'm aware of that," Kevin said, "In fact, she showed up to surprise me this morning. I want you to know, Jack, I had nothing to do with this – it was strictly Emma's idea."

Jack didn't know whether to believe him or not. It might have been because he'd been lying so much himself that his own credibility detector was disabled. At any rate, there wasn't much he could do about it at this point, and he was comforted by the fact that the two lovebirds were unlikely to be discovered.

But later that day, Jack got a call from the detective, who made this report. "So far, I've come up with nothing. But Miss Searles has just taken a trip to London, which struck me as a little sudden. That kind of thing always makes me suspicious. Do you want me to go to England to follow up my instincts?"

Jack mused. *What a spot this puts me in! I don't want to tell him to go, since he would undoubtedly catch the two of them canoodling. I don't want to tell him not to go, since that smacks of impeding his investigation.*

Jack realized (and *Pal* agreed) that he couldn't decide this question – he had to get Cliff Cook involved. He told the detective he'd call him back.

Jack picked up the phone, dialed Cook's number, and repeated to him what the detective said. "What do you think, Cliff? Obviously, there'll be some added expense if we authorize him to go."

Cliff thought for a moment before replying. "Hmm. . . I suppose it's possible she's fooling around over there. That trouble at our subsidiary did seem to come out of nowhere . . . . But she doesn't have any friends in London that I'm aware of . . . . I don't know, Jack. You're my trusted advisor – what do *you* think?"

It was a tough moment for Jack, but (with *Pal's* help) he handled it the only way that seemed feasible at the time. "Well, Cliff, I'm your advisor on litigation matters – not matters of the heart. I think you'll have to make the call on this one."

"Okay," said Cliff. "Since she'll only be gone a few days, tell the detective not to bother. But I'll find out what plane she's coming back on, and you get word to him to check the airport to see if she's flying alone. Then he can resume his coverage back here."

Jack breathed a sigh of relief. Still, he felt a funny feeling in the pit of his stomach, concerned about whether he and *Pal* had done the right thing by his client.

Around noon the next day, Jack received a call from Cliff Cook. His client's voice had a sharper tone than usual. "Jack," he said, "I need to talk to Kevin Dodge about a matter that came up in the early days of the Congruent case, when he was still on our team. It involves something the other side said that I can't quite remember, but it's important – and Kevin, who was there, would probably recall the details. How do I get in touch with him? I called his secretary who said he's out of town – but then she clammed up."

Jack promptly lied and said he wasn't sure where Kevin might be, but that he would find him and relay the need to get in touch with Cook. But Cliff's request, coming out of the blue, made Jack uneasy – although not nearly as uneasy as he felt when, just before hanging up, Cliff said, "Oh, by the way, Jack, I've changed my mind. Have the detective make the trip to London. Emma is staying at the Dorchester. So long."

Jack was stunned. He sat there trying to figure out just how much Cliff knew or surmised, and what to do about it. A few minutes later, the answer appeared at his office door in the person of Jill Marsh.

"Jack, I just wanted to fill you in on something that happened this morning in my meeting with Cliff Cook. Everything about the case itself is fine, but something else struck me as possibly troublesome. At one point, Kevin's name came up. I happened to mention that he was over in London. Cliff seemed extremely interested in the news and ended the meeting a short time later – a little prematurely, it seemed . . . . I hope I didn't do anything wrong."

Jack thanked Jill for her report and provided the necessary reassurance. After she left his office, he sat at his desk pondering the situation with *Pal*.

> *It's clear – especially with the reversal of his decision on the detective – that Cliff has a strong hunch what's going on. And not only in terms of Emma and Kevin – by now he's undoubtedly suspicious of my role in this as well. It would be natural for Cliff to assume that when he told me Emma was on her way to London, I must have known Kevin was over there. The time has come for Pal and me to re-evaluate the situation.*

Jack then decided to put an end to this travesty – to no longer impede the way things play out. But what he quickly discovered was that it's not so easy to extricate yourself from a situation like this without having it appear you've been dissembling from the outset – especially when you have been! "No kidding," whispered *Pal* sarcastically, as he acquainted Jack with the unwelcome fact of life that it often takes a few more lies to unravel the knot.

After some further thought, here's the way Jack saw the situation. He realized he was under no compulsion to protect Kevin and Emma from the consequences of their actions. The only person he had to look out for was himself – and, by extrapolation, his firm, Jenkins & Price. In short, he would now be willing for Cliff to find out that Kevin and Emma were having a fling, as long as this information didn't jeopardize the firm's relationship with Seacrest.

Then, along with *Pal*, he experimented with what he would say to Cliff if he were really to come clean. The *mea culpa* would have to go something like this:

> *I knew very early on that Kevin and Emma were lovers.*

> *When you told me you suspected Emma was having an affair, I withheld my knowledge that she was.*

> *The detective I hired for you wasn't the best available.*

> *When I took Kevin off the Congruent case, I wasn't truthful about another client requiring his services.*

I dispatched Kevin to England to cool things down, so that the detective wouldn't discover their affair.

I didn't advise you to send the detective to London, even though I knew that Emma was over there with Kevin.

When you asked me where Kevin was, I lied again and said I didn't know. . . . Aagh!!!

What the hell, Pal, I just can't say all this to Cliff. I'd look terrible – disloyal to the core. So, the question then becomes, what can I do?

I have to follow Cliff's order and send the detective to London. But I don't have to warn Kevin the detective is on the way – in which case, presumably, he will catch Kevin and Emma in the act. Most important, I have to let Cook know what's going on.

Cliff happened to be out of town that day. Knowing this – and not wanting to get into a telephone discussion with him on the subject – Jack sent a note over to Cook's office by messenger, in an envelope marked "personal". The note read:

"Cliff, to update you, I phoned the detective and told him to get on the next plane to London, to check out Emma at the Dorchester. Then, when I inquired at the firm, I found out that Kevin is also in London. I'm pretty dumb about these things, but the thought has occurred to me that maybe Kevin and Emma are there together. So I reached the detective before he left and told him to also check out Kevin at the Savoy, and to focus on whether the two of them were spending time together. If it turns out my suspicions are true, I'll be mortified. In that event, I apologize fervently to you, both on a personal basis and on behalf of the firm. The problem is, we can't always control our associates all the time . . . ."

Well, to make a long story short, the detective crossed the pond and caught Kevin and Emma together in clearly compromising circumstances. He reported his finding back to Jack by phone. Jack waited until Cliff was again out of the office and then passed the news along to him via another personal note cum apology.

* * *

[Emma musing] *You know, I had a funny feeling Kevin and I were being watched in London. Sure enough, the morning after I got back in town, Cliff came into my office. He barely greeted me, and when he spoke, his voice was very cold.*

"I'll come right to the point, Emma. In recent days, I've suspected you of fooling around with someone else, but I didn't know who. I had Jack Lawrence hire a private detective, who tracked you to London. He saw you in an unambiguous embrace with Kevin Dodge."

I tried to be flip about it. "Gotcha!" *I said.*

"Is that all you have to say?"

"No, it's not, I would also like to state for the record that I can't believe I ever gave my heart to a sick bastard who had the nerve to put a detective on my tail."

Well, it just went downhill from there. I not only admitted the affair with Kevin – I actually went into some detail about the whole thing and how it evolved. I explained how frustrated I'd been by Cliff's reluctance to leave his wife, and that this kind of thing can happen when a woman is resentful. But then my tone changed, and I told him I was prepared to end things with Kevin. I sang a few bars of the Billy Joel song, "Just the Way You Are," to show Cliff I wasn't trying to change him. I even fluttered my eyelashes as an invitation to set things right.

That act has almost always worked for me in the past, so I really wasn't prepared for Cliff's response. But I realize now that affairs of the heart – or, for that matter, of the lower organs – are in some ways like telling lies. You get yourself in deeper and deeper, things get out of hand, and you can never predict where it will all end up.

Cliff's final words came as he turned to leave my office. "I understand your frustration, Emma, although I believe I've been forthright with you from the start – I'm not leaving my wife while my kids are still teenagers. You might give up Kevin, but this kind of affair could be repeated, and I can't handle any more Kevins. So, as of right now, our personal relationship is at an end. And by the way, Emma, you're fired. Arthur Greene, a partner from the Sampson firm, has agreed to come aboard as general counsel, effective immediately. You've got 30 minutes to clear out your things."

* * *

Later that day, Cliff Cook came to Jack's office. They hadn't spoken since Jack sent his two notes to Cliff. His client didn't bother to sit down or even take off his overcoat.

"Just so you know, Jack, I've spoken to Emma and told her I had her tailed by a private detective, who spotted her in London going at it with Kevin Dodge. She admitted their affair."

Jack started to say something, but Cliff waved him off. "She also told me that you knew about their relationship early on – that this was why you took Kevin off the Congruent case and later sent him to London."

Dammit, Jack thought, Kevin must have said something to Emma. You just can't control other people....

"So, Jack, what it comes down to is that you've been lying to me all along. Listen, if you'd told me the truth at an early stage, I wouldn't have blamed you or your firm, because Emma was the person primarily at fault here. Kevin was just a convenient tool for her to use for her own purposes. Hell, even at the end I might have forgiven you as a stand-up guy, if you had come clean and told me the whole sordid tale.

"But lying to me, and then not telling the whole truth when you switched gears – that's no basis for a lawyer-client relationship. How can I trust a guy who's been deceiving me? As of now, all ties of Seacrest's professional relationship with Jenkins & Price are finished. I've already switched the Congruent case over to the Sampson firm – send them the files."

At which point, Cliff Cook turned on his heel and departed Jack's office.

* * *

An hour had passed since Cliff left his office, and Jack was still sitting there dazed. What had him worried now was what he would tell his partners about why the firm got bounced off the Congruent case – especially since he had made such a big deal about it when the firm got hired. He discussed this in detail with *Pal*.

> *I hate the idea of lying to my colleagues, but Cliff's diatribe about my personal conduct being the basis for him firing the firm would not go over well with the partnership. I can just visualize it being used against me when the subject of partner compensation comes up later this year. So, if I'm reluctant to tell my partners the truth, what else can I say to them?*
>
> *One possibility is to blame our dismissal directly on Kevin Dodge, for messing around with the client's girlfriend. When Cook found out, I could say, he was so furious that he took it out on Jenkins & Price.*
>
> *Of course, that will be tough on Kevin. In fact, he's likely to be fired. Even if he stays on, his chances of making partner next year – with this black mark against him – are nil.*
>
> *Under this scenario, I guess I'd have to compound things by lying that I didn't know anything was going on between Emma and Kevin – that when I finally found out, it was too late to save*

the client relationship. *Otherwise, the question will inevitably be asked – if I did know, why didn't I do something about it?*

But do I want to get involved in another round of lies, especially to my partners? Also, I'd be at some risk of being caught in the act. For instance, Cook might relate the real story to one of my young litigation partners – he knows a few of them pretty well.

Kevin is even more of a danger. He's going to be furious over being fired. He might never find out exactly why Seacrest terminated the firm – although if he stays intimate with Emma, she will probably tell him. But even without that, Kevin knows I've been aware of his affair with Emma all along, so he could blow up my story of innocence.

That's why I'm sitting here now in a real dilemma, uncertain of what to do . . . .

Just then, Jack's secretary buzzed to say that Emma Searles was in the firm reception area and would like to see him. Jack, apprehensive but obviously intrigued – *Well, how about that!* – invited her in.

Emma settled herself in an armchair, crossed her legs to reveal a bit of shapely thigh, and stated her business.

"Jack, my sources at the company tell me you've been scolded by Cook and your firm has been bounced as Seacrest's counsel. You may not be aware of this, but I too have been scolded by Cliff – and then not only bounced out of his bed, but also out of my job. So, it seems we have something in common."

Jack nodded but didn't interrupt her.

"Although we haven't conversed much directly, I feel I know you pretty well through our mutual acquaintances, Cliff and Kevin. And it occurs to me that we're really not very different people. I cheated, you lied – it's all pretty much the same thing."

> *Actually,* Jack was thinking, *what I did was a lot more reprehensible than what she did. She's actually giving me a back-handed compliment.*

Emma continued. "I'm a damn good lawyer, as I think you're aware, but I've come to the conclusion that I wasn't cut out for corporate life. So I've decided to relocate to one of the good law firms in town. Jenkins & Price is the firm I know best, think the most of, and could do more good for than any other. And so, Jack, I've decided to ask you for a job. I could come in as a senior associate, and if I proved myself capable, be eligible for partnership in a couple of years."

Jack wasn't expecting this, so he didn't answer right away and immediately summoned *Pal.* A lot of thoughts flashed through his mind in the next few moments.

> *I have no questions about Emma's competence, but based on recent experience, her judgment is certainly suspect. More to the point, though, and assuming she and Kevin are still an item, I'm concerned what impact her arrival would have on whatever spin I decide to put on the reason for our dismissal as Seacrest's counsel.*

Emma smiled. "I think I can guess some of the things going through your mind, Jack. Such as, can she be relied upon – this babe who pats guys on the ass and fabricates a tale to justify going over to London on the company dollar. Look, I can't justify the past and won't try to – but I have learned my lesson, and I'm ready to give my all in this new job at J&P."

> *I nodded in acknowledgement, but she can probably see there's something else on my mind – this woman is very smart.*

"And Jack, there is one respect in which I can be extremely helpful to you. I'm sure you must be wrestling with the question of what to tell your partners about the reason why Jenkins & Price was so unceremoniously dumped as counsel in the Congruent case. Well, I can be your star witness."

Emma spotted the look of alarm on Jack's face, so she quickly added: "Don't worry, I won't rake over the gory sexual details. No, here's what I have in mind. I've been replaced as general counsel of Seacrest by Arthur Greene from the Sampson firm – the same firm that now has taken over from Jenkins & Price as litigation counsel on the Congruent case. I'll just tell your partners that, for personal reasons having nothing to do with my competence, Cliff Cook decided to replace me with Greene as general counsel. And the first thing that Greene did on taking over was to substitute his old firm for Jenkins & Price on the case. This way, it takes the onus off you completely. And there's even a grain of truth in it."

> *This woman is a genius. . . .*

Jack cleared his throat and made a stab at sounding official. "Well, of course you'll have to go through the hiring committee, but I'm sure we'll be able to find a place for you." Then, reverting to his normal voice, he added, "One condition, though – you have to give up Kevin. Otherwise, people who know he was involved in the case originally might put two and two together. . . ."

Emma nodded in acquiescence to Jack's condition, smiled, stood up, reached across the desk to shake his hand, and said, "To paraphrase Humphrey Bogart, as he and Claude Raines march off together to the Free French garrison at the end of *Casablanca*, 'I think this is the start of a beautiful friendship' . . . ."

II

Well, here we are in the Fall of 1978, about a year after Jack's firing from the Seacrest case. Israel and Egypt have signed the Camp David accords, which net Begin and Sadat Nobel Peace Prizes; the death toll from Jim Jones "People's Temple" church in Guyana tops 900 people, including 300 children; and Volkswagen stops production of its Beetle after producing 20 million cars.

And at J&P, things have worked out about as well as Jack Lawrence could have hoped – or did they?

On the basis of Jack's recommendation, Emma Searles was hired by J&P as a senior associate in the firm's corporate department and placed on a two-year track to be considered for partnership. In her interviews with the hiring partners, she managed to work in the "immaculate conception" story of why Seacrest had dumped J&P, in the precise (albeit untruthful) terms she had promised Jack she would use. It was simply the change in Seacrest General

Counsel – which, she says a bit caustically, is "the reason why I'm here interviewing" – that explained the Sampson firm replacing J&P on the Congruent case.

Her story meshed neatly with Jack's own phony version that he told his partners. Nary a word was spoken about sexual innuendoes in either of their accounts – and certainly no hint of Cliff Cook having attributed his decision to replace J&P on the Congruent case to Jack's lies to him.

Still, a tense moment did occur in one of Emma's hiring interviews, when the partner asked if he could contact Seacrest to get an evaluation of Emma from her former employer. Emma, thinking fast, discouraged any such contact, "because of the bad feeling that's been engendered by my ouster." Then she promptly produced written copies of the last few annual performance reviews Seacrest had conducted of all key officers – reviews that rhapsodized over how worthy she was at her job (albeit nowhere alluding to the rumored romance between Emma and the Seacrest CEO). Jack also provided the interviewers with his own favorable opinion of her excellent qualities – omitting, of course, his concern about her good judgment.

Fortunately, the Congruent case was the only "live" matter J&P had with Seacrest at this time, so there was no need to refer to Cook's statement severing "all ties" with J&P. But there remained a pesky question of whether J&P ought to bill Seacrest for the time the firm spent on the Congruent case before being ousted.

The last thing Jack wanted was for J&P to send Seacrest a bill – an act that might well have led to a Cook explosion, rejecting the bill and laying out the whole sordid story. Although Jack had already assured Seacrest that J&P

would waive all of Kevin's hours and also the time Jill needed to catch up when replacing Kevin, Jack hadn't told anyone at J&P about that – figuring it would be buried under the large total fee J&P was likely to receive in the course of a successful litigation. But the charges for his own time – not too long on hours but nevertheless a tidy sum due to his exalted billing rate – were still there.

Jack's solution was to contact the J&P people in charge of billing matters and tell them something along these lines: that because J&P had just gotten started on the Congruent litigation, it would be best not to send any bill – "since perhaps, as a result of our forbearance now, we might be able to get them back as a client some day, if and when the Sampson firm screws up." The J&P billing authorities – none the wiser as to what was really going on – followed his recommendation.

What about Kevin Dodge – how did he fit into all this? Before the firm started interviewing Emma – who had already promised Jack she would "give up" Kevin – Jack advised Kevin that Emma would be joining the firm, "provided you agree not to pursue her any further, or tell anyone what has gone on in the past."

Although Kevin readily agreed to these terms, Jack was frankly skeptical as to how much he could rely on Kevin's word here. After all, Jack reasoned, Kevin would probably assume that screwing a fellow firm associate was far less fraught with peril than taking on the paramour of the client's CEO. Jack managed to assuage his qualms somewhat by the knowledge that Kevin was coming up for partner later this year and thus would not want to allow any embarrassing facts about his recent amatory past to came to the surface.

Still, Jack wondered whether Kevin knew the real story of why J&P had been fired. Although Kevin and Emma would be lawyering in separate departments and thus not likely to come into daily contact, he wondered whether Kevin had been talking to her. (Jack felt he couldn't ask him not to even *talk* to Emma.) And what about the issue of why Kevin was taken off the case and shunted off to London? "Ugh," Jack muttered to himself.

Wait a minute – how about Jill, who was probably suspicious of her being substituted for Kevin, and J&P then being ousted from the case so soon thereafter . . . *Enough already!* – Jack didn't go near Jill and instead relied on her good sense not to raise any of these questions.

* * *

As all this whirled around in Jack's head, he came to the conclusion that he needed someone he could confide in to evaluate his problems and provide him with some good advice on how to deal with them. Sure, the *Pal* he consulted on troublesome occasions was helpful and particularly adept at rationalizing questionable behavior, but Jack wasn't invariably swayed by his advice – which is to say that Jack didn't always trust his own judgment in these matters.

Jack preferred that his new confidant be a lawyer, who would more likely appreciate the complex ethical problems Jack was dealing with, but obviously it couldn't be someone in the J&P firm.

It didn't take him long to decide who was ideal to serve in that role. It was Bob Trent, his buddy from law school days, who was currently a partner in the Smythe firm, another NYC law office of similar size to J&P. Jack considered Bob to be smart, honest, practical, and discreet – just the qualities he was looking for.

Jack phoned Bob, told him of his need for advice – which Bob quickly agreed to provide – and made a date with him for a drink. Seated later that week in their favorite tavern, they began by catching up on each other's personal life.

Bob told Jack about the new weekend house he and his wife had just bought in a distant area of Westchester. Jack told Bob about the sad state of his marriage to Brenda, which had seriously deteriorated in recent months. By coincidence, Bob was having a similar problem. They touched on a few sports highlights – the Yankees sweeping the Red Sox 4-0 in the "Boston Massacre" World Series; golfer Jack Nicklaus winning both the Masters and the U.S. Open.

Jack then proceeded to tell Bob the whole Seacrest story, right up to what was happening at present.

"Wow!" Bob exclaimed as Jack finished his tale. "This is some mess you've gotten yourself into, man."

"Tell me about it . . ." replied Jack wearily. "But let me tell you how those problems affect what I'm doing now at the firm."

During a break, Jack said, "Look, Bob, I really want to stop having to lie or alter facts or duck tough questions – I just want to play it straight up from here on in."

"That's admirable," said Bob. "But let's be realistic. The fact is you've dug yourself into a deep hole here that may make it difficult for you to be clean on the old stuff.

What's vital is that now you work hard not to add to your problems by making new decisions which repeat your mistakes."

"I absolutely agree," said Jack.

Bob continued. "I hope you can see now – and, as they say, with harsh clarity – that in order to hang on to your best client, you got deeper and deeper into a snarl of deception. This is what happens with lies – they breed other lies, and then you begin to tell one thing to one person and something else to another. It becomes tough to keep track of just where you are.

"Not only that, but if you're in a position of relative power – like you are as a partner of the firm – you end up recruiting other people to lie for you in order to perpetuate the deception. You've done just that with your associates. You made Kevin tell Emma he'd been preempted by a non-existent client, who sent him to take imaginary depositions in London, and forbid him from phoning Emma because of nefarious fictional adversaries trying to pin something on him. Even Jill Marsh, the innocent, was made to go along with a lie to support the tale of Kevin's invented long-term client.

"That much is true for anyone in power who lies. For a lawyer, though, it's much worse. You found yourself rooting for the detective to give an "all clear" – so you could transmit to Cook a report that no boyfriend existed – although you knew damn well there was one. And the boyfriend was your own associate! Is that good client service? Is that a satisfactory measure of loyalty?" Bob paused, letting the words sink in.

"I have to say," said Jack, "that those last questions

seem almost rhetorical. . . . Bob, you're going to see a completely changed Jack Lawrence from now on – clean as a whistle."

* * *

Still, it wasn't too long after his conversation with Bob Trent that new challenges of a similar variety arose for Jack. The precipitating cause was that J&P had now begun the annual process of selecting new partners; and – no surprise – one of the prime candidates in the litigation department was none other than Kevin Dodge.

Yes, that's right – the same Kevin who (with abundant help from Emma Searles) caused Jack his earlier Seacrest fiasco. And Jack quickly found out that the current Kevin was not timid about making sure Jack knew of his desire for a partnership – and that he expected Jack to push the firm hard to accomplish it.

Well, Jack could understand this, but it was the way Kevin promoted himself that was vexing. Kevin intimated that if he were passed over for partner, he might be disposed to tell the firm the full story of why J&P lost the Seacrest deal. Jack also detected a hint from Kevin that he might start up relations with Emma, notwithstanding his prior promise to Jack not to do so.

Jack didn't like these implied threats at all – "Who does this guy think he is?" – but he did consider Kevin to be a very good lawyer (making allowances for a lack of invariable good judgment) and had no professional problem lobbying for Kevin to become a partner. Moreover, as far as Jack knew, up to now Kevin had not told anyone what actually happened, nor had he started up again with Emma.

Jack decided to have a chat with Emma, which took place in Jack's office. They hadn't spoken for a while but were on reasonably friendly terms. Gazing at her seated on his couch, Jack couldn't help noting that the hard work and long hours required of a senior associate hadn't dimmed Emma's glamour. They conversed easily on firm matters before Jack came to the reason for the meeting.

"Emma, as far as I know, you have kept your three promises to me: You've maintained the scrubbed-clean story of why J&P was fired by Seacrest on the Congruent case; you didn't tell anyone about your affair with Kevin; and you haven't started up again with Kevin. Am I right?"

Emma replied without hesitation, "Yes, you are."

Jack said, "The reason we're having this conversation is that Kevin is coming up for partner this year, and he's putting pressure on me to get him selected. He has hinted that if he isn't chosen, he might reveal what really happened at Seacrest, and/or that he might start up with you again. I'm not happy about this, as you can guess. Do you have any suggestions?"

Emma thought for a few moments before replying. "Well, first of all, I've worked hard to keep my distance from Kevin, although he's still an attractive guy. Since I don't have Cliff Cook any more, I can be said to be in the market . . . .

"Anyway, although Kevin and I do chat from time to time, we've never discussed this particular matter – although I do know from our conversations how important becoming a partner is to him. But I must say that his threats to you seem a little crude, especially since this is a law firm decision you can't make all by yourself. My personal technique has always been a little more subtle." She paused, and a slight fluttering of eyelashes accompanied her next sentence. "That's something you may notice when I'm scheduled to come up for partner myself next year. . . .

"I'm not sure that Kevin knows the whole story of why J&P was kicked out, and he has to worry that it was all his fault. Even if he isn't selected, he'll know he's better off having the firm give him a good recommendation to move elsewhere. He may even reason that the firm will defer him to a later partner-selection date. I don't think he'll want to jeopardize that.

"As for starting up again with me, I won't let him do that because of my promise to you – especially since I'm coming up for partner myself next year. So I guess he'll just have to find someone else or play by himself . . . ."

Their conversation made Jack feel a little better about the risk from Kevin. although it did cause him to begin worrying about what a handful Emma might become in next year's partnership stakes.

> [Emma musing] *Clearly, I have to hope that my affair with Kevin doesn't come up. It would be harmful enough for Kevin's chances, and I'm rooting for him. But let's face it, it could be even worse for me next year, with all those male J&P partners tut-tutting and turning me down for partnership on strictly prurient grounds . . . .*

* * *

For various financial and administrative reasons, the firm's executive committee decreed that only one new litigation partner could be made this year. In addition to

Kevin, there was another well-regarded litigation associate, Curt Owens, who loomed as a serious current candidate for elevation to partner. It appeared likely that a choice would have to be made between Kevin and Curt.

To Jack, who had worked much more closely with Kevin over the years, the choice to anoint him was clear-cut. Although he was aware of Curt's competence, something about the young man had always bothered Jack. Other corporate partners, however – most notably, George Troy – were very enthusiastic about Curt.

What complicated the situation was that Jack Lawrence and George Troy were viewed in the firm as rivals for pre-eminence in the mid-40's age group. As a result, the partnership prospects of the associates whom each of them supported became an additional arena for their rivalry to play out.

The new partner recommendation committee, which Jack chaired, held a contentious meeting on the subject and ultimately decided to recommend both Kevin and Curt for partner, in order to allow the full partnership to make the final decision. Jack expected some fireworks to erupt at the firm meeting on the subject, to be held next week.
Back in his office after the recommendation committee meeting, Jack took his usual cautionary action. "Hold my calls for the next half-hour, " Jack instructed his secretary over the intercom. He settled himself comfortably in the desk chair and summoned his *Pal*.

"We've got some work to do, *Pal*. The partnership meeting is coming up shortly. I have to decide whether I need to bring up anything about Kevin's affair with Emma when she was at Seacrest."

Apparently drowsy, *Pal* replied in a rare low-key manner. *What's your inclination?*

"I can't help thinking that the incident was serious enough that I ought to report it to the meeting."

Pal appeared to wake up, take a deep breath and start right in.

Look, Jack, we could go back and forth on the issue of just how heinous what Kevin did is. Sure, it wasn't wise, but once you called him on it, he behaved pretty well, and it was really Emma who made things more serious . . . .

But let's face it, Jack, full disclosure here poses a sizable risk to Kevin's chances. Keep in mind all those partners sitting on the fence between Kevin and Curt, looking for a reason to jump one way or the other. Can't you just hear them – "Oh, oh, this shows that Kevin lacks good judgment" – and we both know how that can become the death knell for a potential partner. And for Kevin to lose out to Curt because of this one incident – would it be fair to Kevin, after all his years of splendid toil?

And think of how uncomfortable you're going to be when your partners start questioning you about how much you knew, and when did you know, and why didn't you do something about it.

Jack leaned further back in his desk chair and muttered. "There's a lot to what you say."

And here's one other consideration. Think of how a Curt victory here – orchestrated by George

Troy, Curt's mentor – might affect your relative status in the firm. Right now, you're the standout – esteemed by all your colleagues, who don't know the real reason J&P was dumped by Seacrest. Their respect for you will be further boosted by Kevin's becoming a partner. But that special aura you're presently exuding could evaporate real fast if you can't pull it off.

"I hear you."

* * *

Notwithstanding the "silence is golden" recommendation from Pat, Jack decided he also needed to consult Bob Trent on this issue, which he did the next day in Bob's office.

"Look, Bob, I've already told you everything that happened with Kevin and Emma and Cook and me. I survived the loss of Seacrest as a client, and as far as I know there's been no leakage of the real reason why J&P was canned. But I'm worried that Kevin's partnership candidacy might cause my partners to revisit the whole mess if I reveal Kevin's affair with Emma and where that led. So, the big issue for me is whether, in proposing Kevin for partner, I have to say something to the firm about what happened between him and Emma back then."

They discussed this at some length, including Kevin's implied threats and how Jack's competition with George Troy could be affected by the outcome of the partnership vote. Here's how Bob summed up his advice to Jack.

"You shouldn't lie to your partners about any specific facts. So, for instance, if rumors about Kevin and Emma have reached other J&P partners, and you're asked in the meeting whether they were in fact conducting an affair, you should not feign ignorance but ought to admit that you did know – wherever that ends up taking you.

"But if there's no specific mention of the affair, and you're simply going to recommend that Kevin be made a partner, then you need to evaluate the advice you give your partners on just that point. If you're satisfied that Kevin's coupling with Emma isn't disqualifying, then you can decide not to mention it. You could also decide to mention it in passing, along with your judgment that it's not disqualifying – but of course there's no way to control where that ends up. Anyway, this should be the test – not your own self-interest, or fear of what Kevin might do if he's rejected, or your competition with George Troy – but your own judgment of whether Kevin's affair was potentially disqualifying."

Jack understood the advice but was having trouble deciding which way his own judgment really ran . . . .

* * *

The meeting to decide on new partners of Jenkins & Price was in full swing. The 20 current partners were seated around a large oval table in the firm's spacious conference room. There was a yellow pad and pencil at each place, with pitchers of water and plastic cups in the middle of the table.

Chairing the meeting was Bill Price, 74, head of the firm. The room being slightly overheated, Price and most of the male partners had removed their jackets, but he still wore the vest of his three-piece suit. Bill used eyeglasses, but habitually held them aloft by the earpiece when speaking to a group.

Jack took the floor first in support of Kevin's candidacy, citing the splendid reviews Kevin had received throughout his career at the firm. Then George Troy – articulate, knowledgeable, bristling with self-confidence – made an equally forceful presentation on behalf of Curt. Other partners chimed in, and a lively discussion ensued.

Finally, Bill Price, waggling his glasses, addressed the assemblage. "All right, we've heard from the various advocates for each of these fine young men, and we have before us all the glowing reports on both from over the years. Each has an unblemished record. Just to bring things up to date before we vote, let me ask you, George – since you've worked most recently with Curt – did anything in the recent assignments detract from his prior record?"

"No," replied Troy promptly, "Curt's performance has remained excellent."

"Thank you," said Price. "And now, Jack – I pose the same question to you regarding your experience with Kevin."

Jack had ultimately decided not to bring up Emma voluntarily, but the pointed manner in which Bill Price put the question troubled him. The incident did, of course, "detract" from Kevin's prior record. Could he ignore that in replying?

Pal's voice was right there on his shoulder. *Steady, Jack – remember the big picture . . . .*

Well, thought Jack, I've made my bed. . . . "Kevin has consistently performed quite well."

Price nodded. "I want to thank both of you, George and Jack, for your forceful and instructive presentations here today. Well, that's about it, ladies and gentlemen." Bill Price doffed his glasses. "Let's put this to a vote."

The tally was promptly taken, with Kevin winning 11 to 9.

* * *

As head of the new partner recommendation committee, Jack was the individual who notified new partners of their election. So, shortly after the partners' meeting, he summoned Kevin to his office.

"Kevin, I'm delighted to inform you that the firm has elected you as a partner." Jack rose to clasp Kevin's hand – his delight at Kevin's good fortune mixing with satisfaction over his own personal achievement.

"That's great news," exclaimed Kevin with a big grin. "I was really worried. I knew it was a close call between Curt and me."

"Well, close only counts in horseshoes . . . . I was pleased that there was no mention of what occurred between you and Emma back in the Seacrest days. I think we've kept that pretty quiet. You haven't mentioned it to any of the partners, have you?"

Kevin replied, "No I haven't. But in the interests of full disclosure, I should tell you that back at the time Emma and I were together, I did mention it to one of my associate buddies, Nick Brown . . . . Unfortunately, Nick happens to be a close friend of Curt's . . . ."

* * *

Jack didn't have to wait long. A few hours later Curt came to his office. A sturdily built six-footer, he had a thick shock of dark brown hair, piercing eyes and a deep baritone voice.

"Come in, Curt. Have a seat." Jack summoned his *Pal* to stand by.

Curt balanced on the edge of a chair. "Let me come right to the point. Obviously I'm upset about not making partner. I'd be less upset if I lost out to Kevin in a fair contest. But I learned something today that makes me believe the process wasn't equitable."

"What are you talking about?"

"Nick Brown came into my office to console me after the news about Kevin's partnership was announced to the firm. He said he couldn't believe the partners chose Kevin over me, given the fling Kevin had with Seacrest's General Counsel. I knew nothing about that. He told me the whole story which he'd heard at the time directly from Kevin himself but never repeated until he'd done so today."

Curt cleared his throat. *Pal* took the opportunity to offer a few words of advice. *Say as little as possible, Jack – let's find out what he's got on his mind, and then we can confer on what to do.*

Curt resumed speaking, his tone angry and judgmental. "Based on Nick's description, this was definitely a screw-up by Kevin. Let's face it, lawyers aren't supposed to screw their client's general counsel. I have to assume that the partners didn't know about it – because I'm convinced that if they knew, they never would have chosen Kevin over me . . . . But I think you knew . . . ."

Jack, adhering to *Pal's* directive, didn't respond. Curt went on, his voice rising.

"I'll take your silence for assent. So what I'm saying is that I feel you deliberately withheld vital information from the partners, in order to ensure that your candidate was selected instead of me."

Jack realized he could no longer remain silent. "Now, just a minute, Curt, I think you're going too far here – "

"– Don't try to justify what you did, Jack. Just let me speak my piece." Curt lowered his voice, and the words emerged more slowly. "You know I could cause you and the firm a lot of trouble if I wanted to – such as starting a lawsuit to challenge the firm's selection procedure for making partners. There would be a lot of negative publicity about the firm, and especially about you as the partner involved. . . . But I'd rather not do that. Despite what happened to me, I care about the firm. I haven't told George Troy or any other partner about this. And other than this incident, I have nothing against you personally."

Jack started to say something, but Curt wouldn't allow him to interrupt.

"Let me finish. I also want to make it clear that I'm not looking to have Kevin 'unmade' as a partner. He's a good enough guy, and one screw-up shouldn't ruin his career. But *I* want to be a partner of the firm too, and I think I deserve to be."

He paused to take a breath. Jack waited silently to hear the rest of what Curt had to say.

"Here's what I propose. Why can't the firm make two partners from the litigation department – especially when you have two able candidates? I believe that you – as head of the new partner recommendation committee – can convince the firm to change its thinking and do just that." Curt stood up. "And if you help me become a partner, neither George Troy nor anyone else, will ever hear about this from me, and your reputation will be preserved."

Curt headed for the door, turning back briefly to say, "Think it over. I'll give you the rest of the week to get it done."

* * *

Jack spent a long night in deep discussion with his Pal.

"This is goddam *blackmail*," said Jack, mouthing the word with distaste.

That may be, Jack, but you've got to take Curt's threat seriously. He's angry, frustrated and self-righteous – a volatile combination.

Angry enough to bring a lawsuit? To speak to the media?

I think so – and wouldn't that be a horror show! The legal publications – maybe even the Post

– would eat it up. Imagine all that bad publicity for the firm – to say nothing about how it would affect you personally.

I don't know – his bark might be worse than his bite.

But look, Jack, even if he doesn't sue or talk to the press, you have to figure that Curt will at least complain to George Troy, who in turn will tell Bill Price – and the shit will hit the fan inside the firm.

Jack could envisage a score of indignant partners turning on him – his prominent stature sinking fast, his burgeoning career irreparably damaged.

Besides, Jack, it's difficult to quarrel with Curt's proposal – making a second partner is an elegant solution. That one-partner thing isn't written in stone – it's just an administrative decision the firm could revisit. You can justify it on the grounds that Curt is a deserving candidate and Jenkins & Price will end up better off in the long run – the firm doesn't want to risk losing him.

Jack's resolve was weakening. *Okay, let's say I start the ball rolling toward making Curt a partner. Do I tell everyone why I'm doing that? Do I say, 'Hey, fellas, I'm succumbing to blackmail'.*

No, you can't do that. It would doom the proposal, and then you'd run the risk of the lawsuit, the newspapers, and so on.

How about saying that the idea originated with Curt – after all, it's a very logical request for him to make – *but just leave out the blackmail part?*

Pal thought that one over for a moment. *The problem there is that it'll just seem like sour grapes on Curt's part. If the idea originates with you – his adversary at the partnership meeting, so to speak – it carries a lot more weight. And that way, as a bonus, you can get credit from your partners for a big-hearted gesture toward George Troy's losing candidate.*

Jack was still in doubt. *It pisses me off for the firm to make someone a partner who stoops to blackmail.*

For the moment, *Pal* was reduced to splitting hairs. *Well, Curt didn't actually say he would sue – in fact, he said he'd rather not. So you could argue that technically it's not blackmail, and there are some special circumstances involved here . . . .* Then Pal found his rhythm again. *You might say that Curt is just acting like a savvy commercial lawyer – using the leverage at his disposal to negotiate for a favorable outcome . . . .*

* * *

The next day, Jack settled himself on the small sofa in the office of Walt Young, a key member of the new partner recommendation committee.

"I've been doing some thinking, " Jack said, "and I want to try something out on you before proposing it."

"Go ahead – I'm listening."

"I don't feel good about the Curt Owens situation. He's a first-class lawyer, and I hate to see him leaving the firm because he was passed over in favor of Kevin Dodge. So why the hell doesn't the firm just go ahead and make him a partner along with Kevin?

"Let's face it, a growing firm like Jenkins & Price should be able to afford two new corporate partners. Limiting ourselves to one simply represents an excess of caution – a concern that the good times might not continue. But I believe that's a risk the firm can afford to take, where this kind of irreplaceable talent is involved. If you and the rest of the committee are in accord, I'd like to reopen the issue and push for a second new partner right now."

Walt had been listening to him attentively. "That's a very good idea, Jack. Isn't it interesting how we sometimes lock ourselves into a fixed position and lose sight of our long-term best interests. From time to time, we need to re-examine the limits we've imposed on ourselves, to see if they still make sense. I believe this is one of those times."

"I'm glad you agree."

Walt took a sip of water from a small bottle. "Now that you've raised the idea, it seems so obvious. Did the notion just come to you out of the blue?"

Jack winced inwardly but decided to go all the way down *Pal's* recommended path. "Yeah, it just seemed the right thing to do."

* * *

The next day, Jack convened the new partner

recommendation committee, which quickly endorsed his idea of making a second partner. A meeting of the full partnership to consider the matter was scheduled for the following afternoon.

When the partners had assembled in the big conference room, Bill Price called the meeting to order. "We've reconvened here today to consider the unanimous proposal of the new partner recommendation committee that we reverse our prior position and elect a second litigation partner this year – namely, Curt Owens. In a moment, I'll turn matters over to Jack as head of the committee, but first I'd like to take note of the fact that our newest litigation partner – Kevin Dodge – is with us today, attending his first partnership meeting. Welcome aboard, Kevin." A round of applause greeted the newcomer, who smiled broadly at the warm greeting.

Jack then went through the rationale for calling the meeting – namely, they all hated the risk of losing Curt, they should reconsider making a second partner, business was good, the pro's outweighed the con's. Much of the ensuing discussion was geared to firm economics. The notion appeared to be gaining headway, but some important partners still had reservations – financial soundness, setting a potentially troublesome precedent, etc.

Out of nowhere, George Troy, with a suspicious look on his face, asked Jack this question: "I'm curious what caused you to try to reverse the one-partner decision and wax eloquent over Curt, the guy you were trying to defeat yesterday. Have you been talking to Curt?"

This was a question leading to a discussion that he hoped never to have with the partners. He made a fast trip to *Pal* for advice.

It looks like Curt never told George of his meeting with you, or George wouldn't be bringing up this sore subject. Watch out where you're going here. Just tell 'em a half-truth. Say you had a conversation with Curt and the idea grew out of that. You don't have to get into the blackmail. If you get into the blackmail, you'll have to talk about what Kevin did with Emma.

But Jack, sick of the deceit and having heard enough from his private source, silently muttered, "Get lost, Pal."

He spoke to his partners in a calm voice. "The fact is, I'm proposing the second partner because Curt is blackmailing me to do so – using the threat that if I don't, he'll take some actions that will hurt both me and the firm." Jack then proceeded to relate the details of Curt's visit. This included the fact of Kevin's affair with Emma – but in referring to it in his confession, he didn't identify her by name or as Seacrest's General Counsel but merely noted that she was Cliff Cook's "girlfriend". His voice was determined and forceful as he concluded his remarks.

"Kevin deserves to be a partner of this firm. Curt, if he ever was deserving of a partnership, has forfeited that because of his attempted extortion. And for my misdeeds – withholding pertinent information from my partners, succumbing to a threat to save my own tail, misleading you as to my motives – I deserve to be severely censured."

At partnership meetings, Bill Price rarely acted in peremptory fashion, preferring to let decisions bubble up from the partnership as a whole. Now, however, as Jack concluded his confession, Price removed his glasses and took charge.

"This firm is not making Curt a partner – yesterday, today or tomorrow. In fact, let's tell him exactly how we feel about people who try to blackmail us – and then push him out the door immediately, no matter what the consequences are."

Price turned to look at Kevin. "As for you, Kevin, notwithstanding some apparent warped judgment on your part, you will remain a valued partner of the firm."

Price now pivoted to face Jack. "As for you, Jack, you're absolutely right – you do deserve to be punished. In addition to other consequences that I'll be mulling over in the days ahead – to say nothing of the fact that your partners may never think of you the same way again – there's one thing I'm going to do right here. Effective today, you are no longer chairman – or even a member – of the committee to recommend new partners."

Bill Price put his glasses back on. "And now, ladies and gentlemen, I suggest we terminate these deliberations and get back to productive work."

III

It's now the Fall of 1979, almost a year having passed since that fateful J&P partnership meeting. Iran has taken 63 hostages at the U.S. Embassy in Tehran, Margaret Thatcher was elected Prime Minister of the United Kingdom, and Sony released its first Walkman.

The major event in Jack's life during this span did not involve his profession. Rather, it was that he and his wife Brenda had officially separated and begun settlement negotiations leading to a divorce. The decision to take this step was mutual. For each of them, whatever romance may once have existed in their union had evaporated; and with no children, they lacked considerations of shared parental interest.

Although little acrimony accompanied the separation, Jack was aware that this might change once they got into bargaining over the property split. He knew of other cases where spouses of successful lawyers had sought tough terms that the attorneys felt coerced to accept in order to avoid the kind of negative publicity lawyers dread.

As for Jack's standing at the firm, things were better than he might have expected. To be sure, he'd lost ground by initially failing to come clean about Kevin to his partners. He was able to soften this blow somewhat by a combination of his belated confession, Kevin having gotten off to a good start as a partner, and some profitable new business that Jack brought into the firm. In fact, in terms of his continuing competition with George Troy, Jack probably advanced – George having lost ground by his avid sponsorship of Curt Owens, who had been booted out of the firm for his unacceptable behavior.

Shortly after the partnership meeting in which Jack revealed Kevin's bad judgment, Jack met with Bob Trent and filled him in on what had transpired. Bob was complimentary about Jack's honest admissions to his partners. Bob urged him to replicate that conduct in subsequent situations where good judgment and truthful behavior were requisite.

"I hear you," said Jack. "But I didn't get off scot-free, I was stripped of my committee chairmanship. Bill

Price also alluded to future adverse consequences for me. And he actually told all the partners in the room that they may never think of me the same way again. So I have paid a price for honesty."

Bob replied, "And so it often is. Honesty is the best policy, and it's the one I consistently advocate, but it often carries a price tag."

In terms of Jack's professional demeanor, he had been a relatively good boy throughout 1979 – holding his Pal-driven aggressive instincts in check. He consulted Bob Trent periodically and usually listened to his advice – attempting to play things straight, without deception or the need to lie or misrepresent.

As the year passed, though, Jack became aware that a major challenge for him was coming up in the months ahead. A new crop of associates would soon be nominated to become partners – and among them was certain to be Emma Searles.

Although the two of them worked in separate departments and he hadn't been involved in her assignments since she joined J&P, the indications he received from his partners were that she was doing well and definitely on the partnership track. Still, Jack knew that the upcoming competition could unearth a new set of questions directed to him concerning her Seacrest days, the firm's dismissal from the Congruent case, and Emma's sudden arrival at J&P.

* * *

[Emma musing] *By all rights, I should be made a partner in the upcoming selection process.*

My understanding with Jack when I joined the firm was that this would happen roughly two years out – a time which is about to pass – and I've performed well in all respects.

Still, I've never gotten anywhere by just taking things for granted. My potential weak spot here is two-fold: the fling with Kevin while J&P was representing Seacrest in the Congruent matter, and the lie – well, let me soften that perhaps to "non-disclosure" – that I engaged in when I joined J&P. And let's face it, Jack is the key to both of those aspects.

Kevin did tell me what happened last year with his partnership candidacy and Jack's ultimate disclosure to the firm that Kevin's had screwed around. He assured me that my name was never mentioned – that Jack referred to me simply as "Cliff Cook's girlfriend." Still, I can envision someone who doesn't like Jack – say, George Troy, who's probably thirsty for revenge after what happened with Curt Owens – finding out just who that girlfriend was, and using it against me – or, in reality, indirectly against Jack.

If that were to happen, I wonder how much I'll be able to count on Jack not weakening and telling everyone the whole story, thereby dooming my candidacy. I haven't had much contact with Jack in the past year – maybe it's time to change that now.

What would probably be most useful is for me to do something new that will be positive for Jack – something that would give him a fresh reason to be grateful to me . . . .

* * *

The New Partner Recommendation Committee, from which Jack had been removed, held a meeting and, without opposition, voted to include Emma Searles in its roster of partnership candidates.

Although two other senior associates in her group were also recommended, the firm did not attach any limits this year as to how many partners could be made. The partnership meeting to vote for new partners was scheduled to occur in about one month.

* * *

There was a knock on Jack's office door. He looked up from his desk to see Steven Ames standing there. "Come in, Steven," Jack said at once.

Jack, a litigator, had rarely received a visit from Steven – the foremost J&P corporate partner and a powerhouse in the firm – nor had he ever worked directly with him.

After some small talk, Steven revealed the reason for his visit. "You're probably aware, Jack, that I've been handling the big merger that Anchor Corp. – the firm's largest client – is making of Union Co. But we've just experienced a real hang-up – a lawsuit by a company named Curbside that threatens to hold up the deal. Anchor is anxious that we neutralize this lawsuit as soon as possible so that they can get the Union deal done while the opportunity still exists.

"When I have needed a litigator over the years, I've mostly been using George Troy. But frankly, given that Curt Owens matter, I'm not sure about George anymore.

"Emma Searles, my senior associate on the deal, noticed that I was reluctant about proceeding here with George. So just yesterday she said to me: 'Why don't we get Jack Lawrence to take this lawsuit on – he's a terrific litigator.' As I thought about it, this made good sense, so I'm following her recommendation – asking you to head up the litigation team for Anchor against Curbside."

Jack knew that this assignment would be very favorable to his career, especially if he were able to produce a good result. He didn't hesitate to respond. "I'm honored that you thought of me, Steven, and I'm delighted to accept. Actually, I've heard talk about that problem you've encountered on the Anchor-Union deal, and I have some thoughts on how we might deal with it . . . ."

After Steven left his office, Jack phoned Emma to express his appreciation for her recommendation. He then suggested a time later that day when they could get together, so that she might brief him fully on what was involved in the litigation.

> [Emma musing] *Well, that little assignment gift to Jack should erase any hesitation he might have about making sure I'm promoted to partner....*

* * *

George Troy, still smoldering at Jack Lawrence over the fiasco of his partner candidate Curt Owens, continued to look for payback opportunities. Just such a suitable circumstance arose shortly after he learned that

Emma Searles was being recommended for a partnership.

The opportunity occurred during a conversation he was having with Rudy Kapp, a senior associate who was working with him on a case. Rudy mentioned in passing that he was related by marriage to Arthur Greene, the lawyer who had replaced Emma Searles as Seacrest's General Counsel.

Troy had long suspected that there was more to Seacrest's firing of J&P and Emma's joining the firm than was revealed at the time, but he hadn't been able to dig further into it. He harbored the distinct feeling that if he were to learn more, it would cast a dim light on Jack – a prospect that Troy found very appealing.

Troy knew that Jack had supported Emma at J&P and would undoubtedly be backing her elevation to partner. George reasoned that anything he could do to undercut Emma's elevation would be painful to Jack, an attractive possibility in Troy's mind.

Putting two and two together, George encouraged Rudy Kapp to contact Arthur Greene and try to get the real story of what happened at Seacrest when Emma left.

* * *

At one of their periodic get-togethers, Jack told Bob Trent how Emma had helped him get the plum litigation assignment with Steven Ames. Jack also spoke of Emma's partner nomination, which triggered a pertinent question on his mind.

"What should I do, Bob, if someone asks how Emma happened to leave Seacrest at the same time as J&P

was replaced on the Congruent litigation – and then within weeks ended up as an associate at J&P?"

They discussed it at some length. Bob made his views crystal clear to Jack – namely, that in framing an answer, honesty was always the best policy.

* * *

In the weeks that followed, Jack and Emma spent a lot of professional time together working on the Curbside litigation – in their own offices and at Anchor, but also on some out-of-town trips.

The predictable occurred. No longer restrained by the bonds of matrimony, Jack reminded himself how tantalizing Emma was and did little to hide his attraction to her. From what he knew, she did not appear to be in a romantic relationship; and he assumed Emma was still living up to the commitment she'd made to him to keep away from Kevin Dodge.

[Emma musing] *I'm such a dummy! Here I thought it was so smart to urge Steven to select Jack to head the Anchor litigation team, for which Jack would undoubtedly be grateful. But what I failed to realize is that this would bring the two of us together a lot. And while I continued to think of Jack as my ally in a "beautiful friendship," I ignored Jack's recent morphing into an unmarried readily arousable male.*

I also forgot that even when I don't purposely flirt – and I've definitely tried not to here – I manage to give off vibes that might be taken as showing interest. I've got to stop those fluttering eyelashes! Anyway, the problem is clear – Jack has the hots for me . . . .

* * *

Bob Trent arrived on time at Jack's office for the lunch date Jack had proposed. When he entered the room, Jack was just concluding a meeting with an attractive woman.

"Hello, Bob," Jack greeted him. "Let me introduce Emma Searles, one of our fine corporate associates who's working together with me on a deal. Emma, this is Bob Trent, a partner at the Smythe firm and an old law school buddy of mine – a guy I often turn to for advice when I have a sticky problem."

The three of them chatted for a while about various subjects, including the new *Kramer v. Kramer* movie that they had all recently seen.

After she left, Jack turned to Bob. "I mentioned there was something I wanted to run by you. Well, now you've just met the '*something*'. What can I tell you, Bob – she's beautiful, smart, has a great sense of humor – and let's face it, she's very sexy!

"Aha," said Bob, "you want me to bless a relationship with the woman whose sexual intemperance got J&P fired from Seacrest."

"Well, sort of – or should I squelch these feeling I'm starting to have."

"Hey, Jack, that's way above my pay grade . . . . Why don't you tell me how *you* feel about it."

Jack paused briefly before wading in. "Well, of course it would have been wrong if I were still married. The firm doesn't encourage this sort of thing among its lawyers, but there's no specific negative policy to that effect. Emma and I are in different departments of the firm, which lessens any obvious conflict."

Bob interrupted him. "But Jack, didn't you once tell me that Emma would be coming up about now for partnership consideration?"

"That's true, but the decision whether to nominate her will be made by the partners in her own department. And as you know, I'm no longer even a member of the committee that recommends the candidates."

Bob persisted. "Look, Jack, when Emma came to the firm and protected you by spreading the false narrative as to why Seacrest had bounced J&P from the Congruent case, her expectation was undoubtedly that she'd be made a partner in about two years. Even if you didn't pledge this would happen, I bet you encouraged her in that belief. She may feel you owe it to her to get this done – which means she might be able to exert some extra pressure on that front if the two of you were having an affair."

"Well, I don't know about that . . . ."

"Jack, I seriously doubt the wisdom of you cohabiting with her at any point in time, although let's temporarily defer dealing with the overall question. But for now, at least keep your pecker in your pants until the partnership decision has been made . . . ."

Jack knew Bob was giving him good advice, but – as he later confessed to *Pal* in their colloquy on the point –

whether he would follow it was another question . . . .

* * *

Rudy Kapp returned from his visit with Arthur Greene and met with George Troy, bearing what Arthur labeled as the full and accurate story on Emma and Jack. It had all the pertinent details – Emma as Cliff Cook's mistress, Kevin screwing Emma during the Congruent litigation, Jack lying to Cliff about it – all of which led to Cliff bouncing Emma from his bed and her GC post, and then firing J&P from the Congruent lawsuit.

George Troy listened attentively – taking in the possibilities, assessing his strategy, while rubbing his hands together in glee.

* * *

Notwithstanding Bob Trent's "cool it" caution, Jack continued down the same risky path with Emma – not letting up or putting it on ice even for the time being. With Pal's willing assistance, Jack even worked up a rationale for his decision to let lust overcome Bob's sound advice, which went something like this:

> *I don't know if she'll ultimately reciprocate my feelings. But – and I'll admit I'm a bit ashamed to be having such a nasty thought – I figure the best chance to have her do so is before the partnership vote is taken. Why so? Well, because that's when she's likely to worry that rejecting me might turn me against her, thereby reducing her partnership chances. She may even be concerned that upon rejection I'll name her as having been Kevin's "girlfriend" back then – highlighting that*

unforgivable breach of lawyer-client ethics that the mostly male J&P partners might well penalize her for...."

* * *

[Emma musing] *This is becoming uncomfortable. Jack is getting more tenacious every day. I suppose that's an admirable quality in a litigator, but it's a tough nut to overcome for someone like me who's trying to thwart a romantic entanglement.*

Let's face it, if I turn Jack down cold, there's a real chance he'll take out his anger on my hopes for a partnership . . . . Of course, there's also an argument the other way, namely: If I give in, and word gets out that I'm screwing one of the partners, this would definitely not help my case.

Oh, what the hell – I'm already screwing one of the partners! For the first year, I lived up to my promise not to resume with Kevin. I didn't want to adversely affect his chances of becoming a partner. But once he was voted in, we started up again – although right now we're cooling it for the final months before the partnership vote on me. I probably should feel bad that I broke my promise to Jack, but I must admit I really don't . . . .

* * *

After due consideration, George Troy decided on his strategy. *I'll use Arthur Greene's story at the J&P partnership meeting when they're voting on Emma. Jack is sure to be asked about her* competence at Seacrest – a subject on which Jack gave the firm a strong affirmative recommendation when she came to J&P. *If no one else asks, I'll do so myself.* When Jack confirms his prior recommendation of Emma, I'll then say, "But, Jack, isn't it true that Emma was Cliff Cook's 'girlfriend'". When that comes out, Emma's partnership will come crashing down. She's the collateral damage, but Jack will be the one who's really harmed. Oh yes, and Kevin Dodge too – but I never really liked that guy. . . .

* * *

Jack was jubilant. A key witness in the Curbside lawsuit turned out to be located in Bermuda and unwilling to travel. Jack told Steven that he and Emma needed to go there to interview him. Steven agreed that this should be done.

Back in his office, Jack exulted. *Bermuda is just the kind of romantic venue I need to get over the top with Emma. I can see it all now: after a little mid-day legal work, we take a brisk ride on a motor scooter in the late afternoon, which leads to a romantic swim in the ocean at dusk, followed by a sumptuous supper with a bottle of fine wine – and then I make my move . . . .*

* * *

[Emma musing] *Oh, God, now he's got us going to Bermuda. I know what's on his mind, and I'm afraid I might have to give in . . . . Jack's an okay guy, but I just don't feel the urge to sleep with him. Still, I may have to, if I want to be sure of making partner.*

Then again, maybe I can fend him off for a month – just a little teasing to keep him interested. Once I become a partner, I can then tell him – nicely, of course – "forget it, Jack."

* * *

Rudy Kapp may have been a bit naive when George Troy first told him to pump Arthur Greene for information on Emma Searles, but after he saw how receptive George was to Arthur's narrative, he guessed what Troy was up to.

This disturbed Rudy – mainly because he was a good friend of Kevin Dodge and could see how Greene's revelations put Kevin's actions in a bad light. True, he was aware the partners had been told that Kevin was having an affair with Cliff Cook's "girlfriend," yet they managed to bite their tongues and not treat that as disqualifying of Kevin's elevation to partner. But they didn't know that the "girlfriend" was partnership candidate Emma Searles, then the General Counsel of the company whose case Kevin was actively involved in – which in their minds would undoubtedly have been a much more unforgivable sin on Kevin's part. And who knows where that might lead now, even with Kevin already a partner.

So Rudy decided to tell Kevin what was happening, to warn him that Troy might be up to no good, and to caution that Emma and Kevin were both vulnerable.

Rudy realized that once he spoke to Kevin there was no telling how it would all play out. Troy would probably call him on the carpet for spreading the word. But Rudy decided he was willing to take the heat, even if it affected his own status at J&P. Actually, he was already planning to depart J&P for a good job with a big corporation that had shown interest in him.

After Rudy left his office, Kevin could see the potential damage to his position in the firm. He also faced the decision of whether to tell Emma about what George Troy was likely to do; and there was the further question of whether he (or she) should tell Jack.

* * *

Jack and Emma flew to Bermuda early in the morning. After finishing the day's interrogation of the witness by mid-afternoon, Jack's shenanigans began.

Emma went along with the scooter idea, although she vetoed Jack's insistence that they share a single machine and opted for her own. They enjoyed a swim at dusk on the beautiful beach, where she managed to avoid his roving hands in the deep water. And the supper was indeed scrumptious.

Still, she was fully prepared when he knocked on her door later that night, toting a bottle of expensive wine and two long-stemmed glasses.

Emma opened the door a crack with the lock chain still in place. "Oh, Jack," she whispered in a plaintive voice, "That's such a sweet idea, but I'm just exhausted. Let's save the bottle for a more auspicious time."

Jack protested loudly – she was sure his voice could be heard all the way down the hall – but Emma remained firm, as did the lock chain. Jack had to beat a disappointed retreat back to his room to watch a late movie.

> [Emma musing] *Whew, that was too close for comfort . . . . I hope we can complete the testimony early enough tomorrow to catch a plane back to New York. . . .*

Later that night, Jack sat in a chair in front of the television, turned off the sound, summoned *Pal*, and mused with him.

> *Goddamit, I'm pissed off! I handled everything so nicely – how could Emma turn me down? I'm almost mad enough to threaten her elevation to partner if she doesn't sleep with me."*

> *Pal* joined in. *"Don't threaten her with that. Try something more subtle. She's smart – she'll pick up on it and act accordingly. But listen, Jack, this isn't an idea to run by Bob Trent . . . .*

> *Yeah, I know – Bob would definitely not be in favor of this . . . . And I realize there are potential downsides for me if I play hardball – plus it isn't my style.*

> *I've just got to be more subtle – I'm probably too obvious, and that's what's bugging her. I don't want her to feel that she's levering her way into a partnership through me . . . .*

Jack and Emma completed the witness interview early enough the next day to catch the late plane. Jack tried to persuade her to stay in Bermuda another night, but Emma pleaded the need to get back for some previously scheduled work on the case the next morning.

[Emma musing] *The look on Jack's face as we took our seats on the evening plane made me realize that I'll probably be unable to hold out much longer. I'd better get used to the reality of having to go along with him . . . .*

* * *

And then, only a few days later – with less than two weeks to go before the meeting to select new partners – an unexpected event altered the whole situation.

Emma received a phone call from, of all people, Cliff Cook! There was almost no small talk – Cliff came immediately to the point. He had left his wife; he no longer worried about the reactions of his kids, now older and wiser; and he wanted Emma back in his life, and ultimately to marry her.

Emma, who hadn't spoken to Cliff since leaving Seacrest, was stunned. She thanked him for the call, said she was tied up in a meeting but would get back to him shortly.

[Emma musing] *Well, how about that! – I never thought I'd hear those words coming from Cliff Cook. The last words I remember hearing from him two years ago were, "Emma, you're fired . . . . You've got 30 minutes to clear out your things."*

You know, as I think about it, Cliff isn't really a bad guy. He set me up very well at Seacrest, and spent a lot of bucks on me – and there's a lot more where that came from. And I do have to admit he was justified to be pissed off when he learned about me and Kevin.

The only real problem I ever had was that he wouldn't make the final commitment to leave his wife and bring our relationship out into the open. I was sick and tired of Thanksgivings spent alone munching on a turkey TV Dinner. But now it sounds like the right kind of togetherness for us is finally available.

Plus which, this can get me off this hot seat with Jack. I don't see Jack as the new love of my life; he doesn't have the big bucks I need – and deserve! Jack is smart – he will understand if I go back to Cliff. . . .

I'm actually in a terrific bargaining position with Cliff. He laid himself out bare on his call. I wonder what conditions I can insist on for coming back into his arms. Let's see . . . .

Some points are obvious, but the tough one is whether I'll get my old job back. I really enjoyed being a General Counsel – more than I envision coming my way as a very junior partner at J&P. And that J&P partnership won't even be certain if Jack gets mad at me and decides to reveal all. Even if he doesn't do that right now, the threat still lies there once I became a partner – it could erupt at any time . . . . I think I'll ask Cliff for the G.C. post.

How about being free to fool around . . . ? Hey, kiddo, it's time to grow up – I can't have it all. If I even raise the issue with Cliff, not only will he reject it as a non-starter, but it might cause him to withdraw his proposal entirely.

Still, I'd like to figure out a way to "give this up" in trade with Cliff for what's really important and obtainable – such as the date when we finally get around to marching down the aisle. . . .

Well, that's pretty good for starters. I'm feeling refreshed now. In fact, the words of Gloria Gaynor's big hit song this year come to mind: "I Will Survive". . . . Now let's see what Cliff says.

Emma decided to handle her response to Cliff by phone – she didn't want to muddy the waters with him getting physical in the same room.

"Cliff, I was pleased to hear from you, and your proposal is very tempting. In fact, I'll agree to it if you accept a few points I have in mind. By the way, you may not be aware of it, but I'm about to be made a partner of J&P – so it's not that I don't have other options."

"I'm glad you're receptive to my proposal, Emma. I just stepped out of an ongoing meeting to take your call, so why don't you give me a rough idea of what you want and we can discuss it further when we meet."

"Okay," said Emma. "First, our relationship would have to be public knowledge. I hated the cloak-and-dagger stuff last time. I'd want everyone to realize that we're a couple – that we even spend holidays together.

"I'm okay on this, and I promise to make Thanksgiving a real treat for you."

"Second, no more mini-apartments for me. We would move in together to some plush place and entertain there as a couple."

Cliff replied, "We absolutely move together into a place that's just as nice as where I've been living with Cynthia."

"Third, I don't want to sound petty, but the understanding would have to be that I'm going to be spending real money on clothes and jewelry, and that we get to take trips to exciting places."

Cliff gave a knowledgeable chuckle. "The goodies and junkets will definitely be supplied."

"Fourth, I get my old job back at Seacrest as General Counsel."

Cliff replied immediately. "I thought you might raise that. Emma, and I've given it some consideration. I'd love to have you as General Counsel – I'm not really happy with Arthur. By the way, for some reason he really he dislikes you, but that's a long story for another day. Still, I do have some fear that once our relationship becomes public knowledge, there might be a backlash at the Board level or among stockholders. I'll have to give it some more thought."

Emma replied. "I hear you, but this is a key point for me. Anyway, moving on, my biggest incentive here is the idea that we're going to get married. But I'm concerned about how long that might take."

"Well, Emma, you know it's going to take some time to finalize my divorce with Cynthia."

"I realize that, but I want there to be some incentive on your part to have that time be as short as possible. I'll discuss my thoughts on that when we meet."

* * *

Kevin decided he had to tell Emma what Rudy Kapp had revealed. He told her that Rudy had passed on Arthur Greene's mostly accurate version of their history to George Troy, and that Rudy suspects Troy is likely to do some damage with that information.

Kevin told Emma that he hoped there was some way to fend George off. He said that not only would it be detrimental to her partnership hopes, but it would also turn partners against him for engaging in what they would probably consider reckless and improper behavior.

Kevin mentioned that he hadn't passed this information on to Jack – who, of course, would also be harmed by the disclosure – and he left it up to Emma to decide whether she (or he) should get Jack involved.

[Emma musing] *What awful news! This could be my death knell at J&P . . . .*

Now I'm facing major problems – with Cliff, with Jack, with George Troy, with Kevin, and with J&P. Even for me, that's a little overwhelming. What I really need is someone smart I can turn to for help in deciding what to do . . .

Hey, I know – how about that guy Bob Trent, the one I met in Jack's office. Jack said he often turned to him for advice when good judgment was needed. I think I'll give him a call . . . .

* * *

Emma contacted Bob Trent and asked if he could

see her. She said she knew that Jack relies on him for advice when he has a big problem, and she has lots of problems right now on which she needs some wise judgment.

Bob agreed to meet with Emma without asking what her problems were. Now, as she walked through his office door, he realized he should have found out more in advance. What would I do, he pondered, if the problems involve Jack? Would I have to tell Emma that Jack had previously sought advice from me on how to deal with her?

Emma began their meeting this way. "You're probably wondering, Bob, whether any of my problems deal with Jack. As a matter of fact, he is involved; but before you kick me out of your office, please hear me out. I know you're a good friend of Jack and wouldn't give me any advice that might be adverse to him. But I have learned something Jack doesn't know that could be harmful to both of us. One of the questions I'd like your view on is whether I should tell him about it."

The way she put it made Bob curious to hear what it was, since he then might be able to help Jack deal with it. Bob didn't reveal to Emma that Jack had asked him for advice about his relations with Emma – he didn't want to breach that confidence. But by continuing to listen to her after that opening salvo, he opened the gates; and she felt free to tell him the whole story – including that Jack was becoming more attentive to her than she was comfortable with, and that although she'd told Jack she didn't want to go further, he wasn't slowing down. Then she told Bob all about Cliff, their prior relationship and his recent return to the scene.

"Here's the thing, Bob. I really want to get back with Cliff and ultimately marry him. Actually, right now

I'm negotiating with Cliff the terms of our pre-nup. I know this will disappoint Jack, but I'd like to be able to handle it in a way that is least painful to him. Can you help me?"

Bob could see he was already too deep into this to completely back out. He suggested that before talking about Jack, he wanted to hear more about the negotiations with Cliff Cook. When she raised the General Counsel issue, he told her he did have a view on that.

"Cliff is right to be wary of this, Emma. It's too attackable by someone whose interests are contrary to Seacrest's. You'll be in a good position to advise the company from your position as a J&P partner – don't hamper yourself (or Cliff) with the G.C. title."

"However," Bob continued, "you don't have to give that up right away. I think it may come in handy to drop the demand later in exchange for some items that you want and feel entitled to."

Since Emma had made it clear that she definitely wanted to renew her relationship with Cliff, Bob didn't attempt to plead Jack's case; but he hit on a way to both benefit Jack as well as provide Emma with some additional trading terms to use with Cliff.

Bob said, "If you're otherwise going to have to give up some of what you'd like to get from Cliff, here's an idea of how to trade for it that will benefit Jack. Get Cliff to agree to forgive Jack for what happened on the Congruent deal. Jack still feels terrible about that, and forgiveness could be a big lift to his spirits, which will be further hurt by you rejecting him."

Emma said, "I like that idea."

Bob said, "Make it even stronger by insisting that J&P become Seacrest's prime outside litigation counsel. Actually, that will make sense to Cliff, since you'll be a J&P partner. And make it less theoretical by having Cliff send him some new business right now – something that Jack can boast of to his partners."

The last item on their agenda was how to handle the George Troy problem. Bob was needed for a client phone call and running out of time, so he abbreviated his advice. The key here, he said, is to make Troy feel he has more to lose by this disclosure than to gain if he goes ahead to sully your reputation. As to how to do that, Bob concluded, "You figure it out."

Before she left, Bob cautioned, "Don't tell Jack I'm giving you advice involving him – he might not like the idea."

* * *

Emma and Cliff Cook arranged to meet at a discreet bistro they had often frequented in the past. They sat in a comfortable booth, ordered drinks, and spent the first fifteen minutes catching up on their respective lives for the past two years.

Emma then turned the discussion to the potential future arrangement between them.

"Let me cut to the chase, Cliff. There are three points I want to resolve today – and if they're resolved to my satisfaction, then I'll accept your proposal."

Cliff, said, "Okay, let's hear them."

"First, with regard to the General Counsel point, even though it's a position I would love to have back, I will not insist on it if you have serious concerns about the optics –"

– "which I do," Cliff interrupted –

"and provided we work out my third point, which is related to this. But now let me turn to point two."

"Go ahead."

"Our arrangement has to be clearly premised on the notion that we are going to get married. The wedding should occur within a year. I feel that if you aren't ready to consummate our marriage by then, you've probably changed your mind – at which point I need to be released from any obligation to stay with you" – here she paused for emphasis – "or to be faithful to you."

From the expression on Cliff's face, Emma knew she had made her point.

"But Emma," said Cliff, "we can't get married until my divorce is final, and that may take longer than a year."

"Yeah," she said, "especially if you drag out the financial negotiations interminably . . . ."

"I won't do that. I want the quickest possible turnaround. But sometimes these things do drag out if the other side is relentless, and my wife certainly is inclined that way."

Emma paused to consider this. "Okay, if I feel that you're pushing ahead in good faith for a speedy divorce,

I'll extend the year to the time needed. But our wedding then has to take place within a month after the divorce is final."

They went on like this for a while, but the differences continued to be minimized, and finally both of them were content with the result.

"Okay," said Emma, "now let me turn to the third issue we need to agree on. It involves Jack Lawrence."

Cliff's mouth tightened when he heard Jack's name, and Emma thought she might have trouble with this one.

Emma proceeded to state her case, which can be summarized as follows:

- After splitting with his wife earlier this year, Jack has suddenly gotten attracted to me. So far, I've managed to keep him at arm's length, but he's very persistent and seemingly won't take "no" for an answer.

- Jack is very influential in the firm and has hinted that unless I sleep with him, he may stop being helpful in my promotion to partner – which is very important to me, since I've now signed off on reacquiring the General Counsel post.

- I intend to tell Jack that you and I are getting back together – which I'll cite as the reason why I can't accommodate an intimate relation with him. It's going to upset him, so we need to provide him with something to ease his disappointment and get him in the right mood to actively support my partnership.

- Here's what I've been thinking. First, I know that he remains terribly bothered by you having blamed Seacrest's firing of J&P on Jack having lied to you about my fling with Kevin. Enough time has now passed for you to explicitly forgive him for what he did. It was a mistake on his part, but he meant no harm to you – actually thought he was protecting you. I believe this would carry a lot of weight with Jack.

- Along with that, it would be very helpful for Seacrest to designate J&P as its prime outside litigation counsel. Also, to make that more tangible, please have Seacrest send J&P some business right now, so that Jack can get credit for it in the J&P partnership ranks – as well as end any trace of suspicion from J&P partners as to Jack's role in the Seacrest firing two years ago.

Cliff balked at this initially – and had some choice words for Jack – but over the course of a second drink, plus some alluring fluttering of Emma's eyelashes, he grudgingly agreed to Emma's proposal. The deal was sealed with a shaking of hands and, more to the point, a warm kiss.

[Emma musing] *Well, that wasn't too bad – Cliff's buttoned up. Now I've got to deal with Jack, which shouldn't be that much of a problem. Cliff's arrival on the scene gives me a perfect alibi for not succumbing to Jack's advances, but also creates some plusses for Jack that I've gotten from Cliff. Of course, there's still Troy on the horizon – that one is unlikely to be so easy. . . .*

* * *

Emma entered Jack's office and began speaking even before she sat down.

"Jack, guess what? Cliff Cook just came back into the picture! He split from his wife and wants to re-ignite our relationship, only this time more seriously – going all the way to marriage! I've worked out the terms of the arrangement with him, and frankly, this is a proposal I just can't turn down."

Jack appeared stunned by the news and didn't reply right away. So Emma continued. "You're a great guy, Jack, but you can't match this trip for me into the world of ultimate luxury that I've always dreamed of. And frankly, it wouldn't have looked good for two partners – I'm expecting that I'll soon be anointed – to be cohabiting." She paused briefly to consider whether it was wise to voice the next thought, but soon concluded, what the hell . . . . "Maybe it's even worse than starting up an affair while someone is being considered for partner."

Jack still didn't venture a reply, so Emma kept going. "Jack, you've been a great supporter of mine, for which I'm very grateful. I told Cliff that I wouldn't go with him unless you were taken care of in some meaningful way."

Now she had Jack's full attention.

"Cliff understood the point. I mentioned that it still pained you for Cliff to think you'd lied to him about Kevin and me – that you had just been trying to protect Cliff from the bad news. Cliff thought about that for a minute and then said, 'How about if I tell Jack that I forgive him for what happened back in those difficult days. And to prove that,' he said, 'I want to reinstate J&P and Jack as Seacrest's prime outside litigation counsel going forward'."

Emma saw a change of expression in Jack's eyes at this news. *It just goes to show,* she thought, *the truth of that old adage to the effect that you can get almost anything good done as long as you're willing to give the credit to someone else.* But then she decided to complete her presentation in a way that would entitle her to at least a piece of the credit.

"I told Cliff that I was sure you would appreciate this, but that I felt he ought to make it more tangible by sending J&P some immediate business for you to work on – which he promptly agreed to do. . . .

"Jack, I need to excuse myself for a few minutes to take a call I'm expecting. It'll give you an opportunity to reflect on this. But again, thanks for everything."

After Emma exited his office, Jack closed the door and summoned his *Pal* to ruminate on what he'd just heard.

Well, sure I'm disappointed that I can't get my hands on this exciting woman. But I'm a realist, and I can't compete with what Cliff Cook has to offer.

I also have to admit that the point she made about two partners consorting has merit. It's just the kind of warning that Bob Trent made to me. . . .

And Cliff's willingness to forgive me for what happened two years ago – an incident that still rankles – is really great news.

Here *Pal* broke in. *Nice vibes, to be sure. But what I really like is reinstating J&P as Seacrest's prime outside litigation counsel – that's tangible. And sealing the deal with some immediate business you can point to with your partners – terrific!*

Jack added, *Plus which, Pal, once Emma is a J&P partner – which I'll help her to become – and is bedded down with Cliff, all the more reason for J&P to get Seacrest's business.*

Just be careful, said Pal, not to get into any of that past history during the partnership deliberations. Also, Cliff and Emma should hold off any public display of affection until after Emma is elected. Otherwise, some people might put two and two together and recognize Emma as Cliff's "girlfriend" that Kevin was in bed with . . . ."

When Emma returned to Jack's office a half-hour later, Jack spoke in a positive tone. "I understand this, Emma; and although I'm personally disappointed, I realize you've chosen a wise course yourself, which also has some benefits for me. Congratulations – and now, let's make sure you become a partner."

"Thanks, Jack, for seeing the reality in all this." Now she introduced the other problem that she purposely hadn't referred to up to now. "Jack, I need to tell you of another recent development that might pose a significant obstacle to my partnership unless we figure out a way to handle it."

Emma took a deep breath and revealed to Jack what Troy was up to, based on the warning Kevin received from Rudy.

Jack quickly realized that this was a serious concern. He was aware that Troy had it in for him and would look for ways to bring him down. It might cost Emma a partnership, but could also be harmful to him. Jack could just imagine the fuss if his partners were to hear that J&P was sacked by Seacrest because Jack lied to Cliff – and further that Jack lied to J&P (with Emma's help) about what really had caused the loss of Seacrest as a client.

It was clear to both Emma and Jack that they needed to block George Troy from making these disclosures at the partnership meeting. But it wasn't obvious how they could accomplish this.

The troubling aspect here was that Troy wasn't just inventing something negative. He was, in fact, in possession of the truthful facts about what happened back then. Unless they could shake George's confidence in the accuracy of what Arthur Greene had told Rudy, they had few weapons to use against Troy. But to cast serious doubt on its veracity would require them to do something that neither of them was anxious to undertake . . . .

* * *

At the end of the day, a memo was circulated to the partners reminding them that the partnership meeting to decide on new partners would be taking place in two days.

* * *

The following morning Jack and Emma were seated

in George Troy's office. "Why are you two here?" asked Troy.

Jack replied. "We got word that Arthur Greene has been peddling a phony story about how J&P lost the Seacrest account – a story that implicates me and could also have a negative impact on Emma's partnership expectation. I understand that you've gotten possession of this false narrative."

The die was cast. Even though Jack had promised Bob Trent that he wasn't going to lie anymore, he was doing it now – a decision with which Emma was totally in accord.

Emma now spoke up. "What you undoubtedly don't know, George, is that Arthur, who succeeded me as Seacrest's General Counsel, has long been hostile to me." As she spoke, Jack thought to himself, *well at least that part is truthful* . . . "Now that he has learned I'm coming up for partner at J&P, he's spreading lies to sabotage my chances."

"What a minute," interrupted Troy, "I can't see how –"

Jack ignored Troy's anticipated pushback and picked up their message. "We just want to warn you, George, not to repeat any of this nonsense that Greene is spreading, or do anything else that would sabotage Emma's partnership chances. If you do, we will not only deny Arthur's lies, but I will also let the J&P partners know that you're doing this dirty trick just because you don't like me, and you think that sabotaging Emma's rightful partnership expectation will hurt *me*."

Of course, Troy strenuously resisted all aspects of their story. But Emma could see that George was aware of how angry Jack had gotten over this – a realization that gave some teeth to Jack's threat to reveal George's nasty motive. She also reasoned that Troy doesn't know Arthur Greene – so would he really want to rely on what Greene says, especially if Arthur has it in for his predecessor G.C. . . . .

The meeting ended inconclusively. Rehashing it later in Jack's office, he and Emma found it hard to predict what Troy would do at the partnership meeting.

* * *

The meeting the next day to select new partners was in full swing and the individual now being considered was Emma Searles. Those who had worked with her spoke affirmatively about her abilities. George Troy hadn't said anything so far, nor given any indication whether or not he would try to expose her. Presiding partner Bill Price now called on Jack.

"Jack, I know you had some contact with Emma while she was Seacrest General Counsel and you were working on their Congruent case. Do you have any observations to offer us from those days that would be pertinent to our consideration of Emma for partnership?"

What went through Jack's mind at that instant was the question of what he would say if he were to tell the truth – that Emma was smart and practical and a lot of other good things, but she had exhibited some of the worst judgment in terms of her behavior with Kevin that he'd ever seen in a general counsel . . . .

Pal made a quick appearance with a warning: *Careful now, Jack. Don't hold back positive comments because you're worried what George might have up his sleeve on the subject. Speak affirmatively, and don't worry about Troy.*

"She was very impressive," said Jack, "as I told you all when she first came into the firm. Definite partnership material, and I think her performance here has well borne out that prediction."

"Thank you, Jack," said Price, "Does anyone else want to comment on Emma before we take a vote."

"Yes," came a voice that Jack instantly identified as that of George Troy. "I'd like to ask Jack a question about Emma."

Here it comes, thought Jack – *and I'm not really sure how to handle it. But let's face it, there's no way it's going to be good....*

"Jack," said George, and the look in his eyes foretold the worst, "just one thing."

"What's that?" said Jack, trying to inject some quiet menace in his voice to warn Troy about the potential adverse consequences to him of meddling with Emma's partnership.

George paused a moment and then spoke, "Did Emma, as a corporate lawyer, appear to appreciate the litigation aspects of the case?"

Whoosh came Jack's exhalation of breath, as he realized the crisis was past.

"Absolutely, George" he replied. "She grasped the situation well and offered some helpful observations . . . ." Troy and Jack looked at each other with a great deal of menace in their eyes that belied the inoffensive words on their lips.

A few minutes later, the vote taken in favor of making Emma a partner was unanimous.

* * *

The afternoon after the partnership meeting, Emma met with Kevin. She told him the unvarnished story of how they had discouraged Troy from using Greene's "story." Kevin was happy about that – not only for Emma, but also for himself.

"Kevin," said Emma, "there's one more thing I have to tell you about. Cliff Cook has now come back into the picture, bereft of his wife. He wants me back – all the way to marriage – and I'm going along with it." She paused. "I hope you can understand why."

Kevin said, "I do understand, and I congratulate you on that development."

Emma replied, "Yes, I'm riding high now. Sort of like the city of Pittsburgh, whose football Steelers won the Super Bowl and whose baseball Pirates won the World Series, both this year . . . Now if President Carter can just get those hostages out of Iran . . . ."

Kevin smiled and then said, "What does that mean for us? I was certainly hoping we would get back together after you had been made a partner."

"Kevin, I tried my best to get Cliff to go along with an extracurricular social life, but he absolutely forbid me to even think about it. He says he's intent on our getting married as soon as his divorce is final."

"That's too bad," said Kevin. "I've really enjoyed our time together."

"Me, too," said Emma – and then, after an intentional pause, "Well you never can tell . . . ."

* * *

Alone now with *Pal*, Jack rehashed the whole thing, concluding *that it would have been wonderful to connect with Emma, but I can see she's in better (or at least richer) hands with Cliff.*

Jack wasn't proud of what he and Emma had done to discourage George Troy from his vendetta. He tried to think of another word than "lying" for the process, but was unable to come up with one. The best he could do was rationalize his behavior with this concept: that Troy was going to do the wrong thing, so what he and Emma had done had been the right thing – but he didn't find that thought completely satisfying.

Pal, however, was ready to move on. *Anyway, I think you should shelve any idea you may have had – and I know you referred to this in one of our chats – to split the credit with Emma for J&P getting back the Seacrest business. As far as your partners ought to be aware, this was all due to your re-establishing direct relations with Cliff Cook.*

"Okay, *Pal*, I'm with you on that. But the question I still have is whether all this will work out down the road? Or will new problems emerge from what we've done up to now that bedevil us some more?"

Pal reflected on this for a few seconds and then said, Look, what's happened up to now, and solving yesterday's and today's problems, make for a damn good novella. But let's face it – trying to solve tomorrow's problems would definitely require a novel....

Jack smiled and nodded his head. Then he mused: *You know, Pal, everyone around here – me, you, Emma, Kevin, Troy – we all have a little dishonesty in our hearts. There are very few completely straight and trustworthy people – very few Bob Trents....*

* * *

A week later, Emma invited Bob Trent out to lunch to thank him for his advice over the past month and also for his refusal to charge her a fee for his services.

They were seated at a corner table in a high-class restaurant. Emma was clothed for the occasion – projecting a much more provocative look then she did in the corridors of J&P. As must have been apparent to everyone in the restaurant, Bob had visibly melted in the wake of the total charm offensive that Emma had launched his way.

At one point, Bob asked Emma how she had managed to discourage George Troy from trying to ambush her partnership quest. Emma, speaking out of the corner of her mouth in imitation of how a mafia don might have replied, said simply: "We made him an offer he couldn't refuse." But she declined to get into a description of just what had gone on in the meeting that she and Jack had with Troy.

Bob mused to himself. *I just can't understand why Troy backed down. He had the accurate information, plus the harmful motive. What made him back off....?*

When they finished dessert, Bob said, "Emma, I was pleased to advise you. I wish you well in your marriage with Cliff Cook. And I hope you'll turn to me any time you need further advice."

Emma smiled, reached across the table to take Bob's hand, and said: "To paraphrase Humphrey Bogart, as he and Claude Raines march off together to the Free French garrison at the end of *Casablanca*, 'I think this is the start of a beautiful friendship . . . .'"